THE DRUMS

THE DRUMS

MIKE JOYCE

new modern

new modern

First published in the UK in 2025 by New Modern
An imprint of Putman Publishing
Mermaid House, Puddle Dock, Blackfriars, London, EC4V 3DB

@newmodernbooks
@newmodernbooks

Hardback ISBN: 978-1-917923-22-4
eBook ISBN: 978-1-917923-25-5
Audio ISBN: 978-1-917923-24-8

A CIP catalogue record for this book is available in the British Library.

Publishing and editorial: Pete Selby and James Lilford
Typesetting: Marie Doherty

3 5 7 9 10 8 6 4 2

New Modern is an imprint of Putman Publishing
www.newmodernbooks.co.uk
www.putmanpublishing.co.uk

MIX
Paper | Supporting
responsible forestry
FSC
www.fsc.org FSC® C018072

Printed and bound in Great Britain by Clays Ltd, Elcograf S.p.A.

In memory of a true one in a million – Andy Rourke

Dedicated to Tina Bee

CONTENTS

Introduction   ix

Part 1: BEGINNINGS

1   Manchester, Irish, Working Class: *1963–1976*   3

2   Kid of the Croft   11

3   Our Lord   17

4   Social Meat   23

5   Smells Like Fruit   27

6   A Crack on the Head   33

7   Mr Romantic   37

8   Ever Fallen in Love: *1977–1978*   45

Part 2: BECOMING

9   Fick as a Brick: *1978*   53

10   A Different Kind of Frontman   61

11   International Star   67

12   Adulting (Kind of)   73

13   Victim: *1980–1981*   79

14   Steven and Johnny   83

Part 3: THE SMITHS

15	First Gig: *1982*	93
16	Andy	99
17	So It Begins	105
18	'Hand in Glove'	117
19	Rough Trade	121
20	Touring, Touring and More Touring	125
21	John Peel	131
22	Cannock Chase	135
23	The Birth of Morrissey	139
24	*The Smiths*	143
25	The Haç AND *Top of the Pops*	149
26	Englishmen in New York	157

Part 4: HOW SOON IS CELEBRITY?

27	Band Life: *1984*	165
28	Making *Meat is Murder*	177
29	No. 1: *1985*	189
30	*The Queen is Dead*	205
31	Craig	209
32	American Dreaming	215
33	*Strangeways, Here We Come*	237
	Epilogue	247
	Acknowledgements	253

INTRODUCTION

O nce you're in a band, you're in a band. Even when you're not on stage, you're in a band.

People ask me all the time, 'What's Morrissey like?', 'What's it like to walk out on stage at Glastonbury?' or 'What's it like playing concert venues up and down the country, a little indie band selling out the Royal Albert Hall?' And my answer is always the same: it's unfathomable. What we achieved, how we touched people's lives, was just not within the reach of most bands, let alone your average human being. You might be in a band and that's cool; but to do what we did? It was unique. It's hard to explain what it's like to see people in a crowd just *crying*, people who don't know each other, shaking through the sheer emotion of what they have collectively experienced. It could be frightening. Like a religious awakening. A possession almost. If you can do that in a fucking band? Well, that's pretty rare.

For more than forty years now, being in the Smiths has defined my life. Everything comes back to us as a foursome, even when it probably shouldn't. Being in that band gave me a different perspective on every aspect of life; people treat you differently, from random strangers on the street to your closest family and friends.

When my son Frankie was at school and had exams coming up, I tried to explain to him that he needed to work hard, study and put in the effort because the options weren't going to be great if he didn't.

He looked at me indignantly and said, 'What did you do, Dad? Didn't you tell me that you didn't even bother going in for the exams and left school at sixteen?'

I said, 'Yeah, but I was in a band, I became a *Smith*, so it was different.'

I remember speaking to my careers officer when I was fifteen or sixteen. Back then, you were assigned a meeting to speak about your future, discuss what you think you're going to do with your life, how best to exploit whatever formal qualifications you may or may not have achieved. I went in, being Mr Billy Big Bollocks, saying, 'I don't need any qualifications. I'm going to be in a band!'

He said, 'Do you know what the guy who came in before you said? He wanted to be a lion tamer. I think you're probably in that same boat. I'm putting him down for council work and I'm putting you down for council work too.' 'Council work' meant manual labour on the roads of Manchester – it was the starting point for any career if you weren't academic. Without a flicker of a smile, I was dismissed as he snarled, 'Now, get out!'

The funny thing about that meeting is I bumped into the same guy about twenty years ago in Tesco. He came up to me, slapped me on the back and exclaimed, 'Mike, you did it!'

I said, 'Yes, I did, didn't I?'

He replied, 'I could not believe it. I was sitting watching *Top of the Pops* with my wife and I said, "There's that lad, Mike!" It was the first time I had been so wrong about what I felt sure was just some pointless dream.'

I smirked at him and shrugged. I had achieved my goal. I *was* in a band. But being in a band like the Smiths was like winning the lottery.

For the five years that we were together, me, Andy, Johnny and Morrissey were in such a unique position that we became an incredibly tight-knit unit. You can't speak to your mates, family, friends or anybody about it because they don't know what it's like. Nobody does. It's the siege mentality of being in a huge band. It becomes very insular because nobody else can truly comprehend it.

When one of us would say to one of our non-band mates, 'Yeah, it's really exhausting being on the road,' they would respond snarkily with, 'Yeah, I'm sure it is, when you got a number-one album, you get to go on *Top of the Pops* and you just played in front of 20,000 people. Poor fucking you!'

When looking at the timeline of the Smiths, sometimes people say, 'Well, considering you were only together for such a short period, you shone brightly.' When you study the logistics of what we did within that four years we were together, they were right. Some bands only release one LP in that sort of time frame. We had eighteen top forty hits. All we ever did was work. We released a single every two months, went out on tour, then recorded an album. Then just repeated that process. It was absolutely relentless.

Even when we weren't doing shows or undertaking band-related duties, we were hanging out together. I saw Johnny pretty much daily from 1983 to when we split up. Every single day, seven days a week, we'd go and smoke a bit of dope, play guitar or listen to music and watch TV.

For me, playing music is like having a conversation with somebody. That's something that's always put me off taking on any session work. Don't get me wrong, I don't have anything against session players, but for me to have a bond with somebody musically, I've got to have a connection with them before we even start playing. That gives me a better understanding of where they're at, how they function and who they are as a person.

The Smiths were a very standard line-up: bass, drums, guitar and vocals; let's not forget that musically we were only a three-piece.

So, what made the sound of the Smiths so unique? Well, having one of the best songwriters Britain's ever produced in Johnny certainly helped. Likewise with Morrissey's idiosyncratic approach to lyric writing. But I'm talking about the *sound*. Couple those two with mine and Andy's contribution and that's what made the *sound* of the Smiths; it is what made the Smiths what they were. One can argue that Johnny or Morrissey, or a combination of both *were* the Smiths. But I'm of the opinion that the actual *sound* that you hear when you listen to every song that Andy and I played on during the lifetime of the band *sounded* like that because our individual style of playing contributed to the overall finished composition you hear. That is undeniable. Without taking anything away from Johnny and Morrissey's brilliant and distinct writing abilities, their solo work *sounds* nothing like the Smiths. Obviously, they're not trying to be the Smiths. But that's not the point I'm trying to make. They couldn't sound like the Smiths because of the particular contribution Andy and I brought to the table.

There was an album that came out recently, some 'Best of the '80s' compilation. The Cure were on it, the Human League, ABC, Culture Club, Depeche Mode and every single fucking band that was something in the '80s. The Smiths were not included. I took that as a compliment because even though we were happening right in the middle of the '80s, we had nothing musically to do with that decade. We could have been from the '60s '70s or the '90s. It was timeless. We could have sat anywhere. We sat aside from the feel and fashion of the '80s. And that timeless influence of the band is reflected in our popularity right up to the present day with the TikTok and Gen-Z kids. I was DJing in Margate last year and the guy who picked me up asked if I was on TikTok. I told him I wasn't, so he showed me all the references to the Smiths on the platform, from a mariachi band covering 'There is a Light That Never Goes out' in South America to an assembly of primary-school children singing 'This Charming Man' in Jakarta.

Even now, I find the whole Smiths 'thing' hard to compute. Once, when we played in Boston, we went off stage before the encore and I had to go to the loo before we came back out. There I was standing in the bathroom, quickly going about my business, hearing the 15,000 kids in the audience chanting, 'Smiths, Smiths, Smiths' – *15,000 people cheering that name.* It sounded pretty fucking mega, trust me.

I'm tapping my foot while I'm having this piss. I'm getting dead excited thinking, *Well, right, I'll have to go out and see this amazing band because they'll be coming on in a minute.* Then I realise – I'm *in* this band. I'm in the band that's been chanted for by 15,000 crazed American kids. I'm playing drums with my friends and performing the music that we created. All I'm trying to do is to make the show as great as possible, to do my bit as one corner of this incredible square. And as long as Johnny, Andy and Morrissey are happy, well that's good enough for me. But 15,000 screaming American kids? Yeah, it helps.

That's not to say that everything was perfect all the time, but my overwhelming memories of the band are hugely positive. Maybe it's just because *I'm* a naturally positive person. Life is not always fabulous, but what I try to do during difficult times is accept the issue then look for the upside. I will always find that silver lining, regardless of how faint it is. The light at the end of the tunnel can be magnified; that helps when dealing with bereavement or with a situation that seems unbearable or insurmountable. Or, as the years pass, with old bandmates.

I don't mean papering over the cracks, pretending that something hasn't happened or belittling moments of gravity. I saw a quote from Ian Brown – the lead singer of the Stone Roses – that really summed it up for me. I paraphrase: 'It's better for it to have happened for a short time than never happened at all.' That's how I try to face things when somebody dies or something seems to go wrong. I think, *Let's celebrate the fact that we had that person in our lives or we had that experience with that person, the joy that was brought by that individual in relation to all of us.* I try to concentrate on the beauty, not the demise.

Over the years, there has been a lot of stuff said about the issues in the band and the legal disagreements after the Smiths disbanded. There are plenty of encyclopaedic accounts of what happened and what didn't happen. There are plenty of fictional accounts too. But I have little desire to dredge this up again. Everything that needs to be said has been said. When I look back, as a pragmatic and content man in his sixties, I choose to focus on the amazing highs of being part of the band. I want this book to be a love letter to that time and a love letter to the Smiths, capturing some of the stories and moments that defined that period of my life for me.

I'm not a nasty person and I'm not snide. I would never want to hurt anybody ever in my life for anything. I'll go out of my way to make sure people are happy and at ease, even if that takes me out of my comfort zone. Maybe having a good life is payback for that.

I seem to be lucky in everything that I do, but I'm a firm believer in the idea that you make your own luck.

As a musician, all you can do is your best. Whether it's a drum part, a bassline, a guitar part, a lyric or a vocal melody, you just create the best thing that you think is right to serve the song. That's all you can do.

As Andy and I used to say, 'Where did it all go right?'

After all, I was just a lad who played the drums.

PART 1
BEGINNINGS

1

MANCHESTER, IRISH, WORKING CLASS

1963-1976

It was a dangerous and dark place, Manchester. The buildings were black with soot, giving everything a grimy, used-up look. It was a very closed city, very parochial. I don't think people realise that now; it wasn't particularly welcoming. You didn't come to Manchester to visit, you didn't come for your holidays, you didn't come to have a look at the city centre for all it had to offer because it had nothing to offer. It wasn't a utopia. Once the Smiths got signed, we were out for a meal in London with our record label Rough Trade. I was seated next to someone I hadn't met before. I told him that I was from Manchester and the expression on his face was a mixture of disdain and pity. He turned away, completely uninterested. I was from an alien land; I'm different because I am from Manchester. There was no connection. I was of the frozen wasteland up north.

Manchester is a strange place because, normally, within a city's environs, people move to the land that's not central to the city itself. They start to occupy space that gets progressively further and further away from the centre, fleeing the unrelenting metropolis for the breathing space of quieter, greener suburbs. Manchester is the other way around.

People have gravitated *towards* the middle more and more over the years; with the new skyline of skyscrapers, it's now earned the charming title of 'Manc-Hattan'. Areas like the Northern Quarter are now full of hip record stores, bars and restaurants – that is not how it was when we were growing up. Those places were no-go zones.

I loved it and hated it at the same time. I had no affinity with the place. I found it quite oppressive, especially when I was younger and was trying to find my feet. Become my own person. An individual. Anyone bohemian, arty or into music was viewed as strange. Such things were simply not allowed. We were weirdos, freaks and outcasts.

Mam and Dad had come over from Ireland in the 1940s. Mam started life in Portalington, County Laios, in the midlands, west of Dublin; her father had originally moved to the UK with a few of his siblings who settled in the north west. Mam's family, in terms of numbers, was your typical Irish Catholic 'double figures'; Dad's was not far off. He came from good farmer stock in Shrule, County Mayo on the west coast. He arrived in the UK at about the same time as Mam, looking for employment. Dad would take on any job that was available, though he found himself most often engaged in the building trade.

Mam and Dad, 1950s.

When my mam first arrived on British soil, the Second World War was raging. She found a job in a factory building Lancaster bombers. Growing up, I remember her working two, sometimes three jobs to make ends meet. She'd spend her mornings at the Princess Hotel in the Mancunian borough of Fallowfield, cleaning and preparing the rooms, before going to the home of a rich family at the far end of Wilbraham Road in south Manchester, where she was employed as a maid. She would then come home and make everyone's tea before, finally, going for her shift in the cloakroom at St Kentigern's Social Club. She also worked at the prestigious Midland Hotel in central Manchester with her sister, waiting on tables. She was always doing anything she could to bring money into the family.

One story that was part of Joyce clan lore happened when Mam was working at a New Year's Eve party at the Midland and the guests consisted mainly of US servicemen and women. Part of my mam's role was to lay and decorate the tables; as it was Christmas, this included placing a huge cracker at each setting. She was beckoned over by a GI who told her that they had already opened the massive Christmas cracker that was supposed to be pulled at midnight – would it be possible for Mam to get them another? She nodded, gave him a sort of curtsy, then went and retrieved a replacement for him. After she put it on the table, he grabbed her hand and said 'Thank you', placing a piece of paper in her palm. She went into the kitchen and had a look to see what it was, expecting it to be a message. But it wasn't – it was a £5 note. Mam said she'd never seen one before. I've just had a look and, in 1940, £5 would be worth a little more than £350 in today's money. That's not a bad tip, eh?

Both my parents worked every day of their lives, regardless of how menial the role, toiling all hours to feed us kids. The mindset was to pay the rent and clothe the children; that was as far as aspirations went – within the Joyce family, anyway. Nobody was signing on or receiving benefits; to take any sort of hand-out was considered quite shameful.

Irish people are not workshy. Because of this strong work ethic, if you weren't in employment, you had to have a very good reason why. It simply wasn't the done thing to receive unemployment benefits and sit around unless you were ill, disabled or dying.

X

I was born at home on 1 June 1963. Instead of a cradle, I was unceremoniously placed into a sock drawer. No point in having a cot when a drawer with a blanket in it will do.

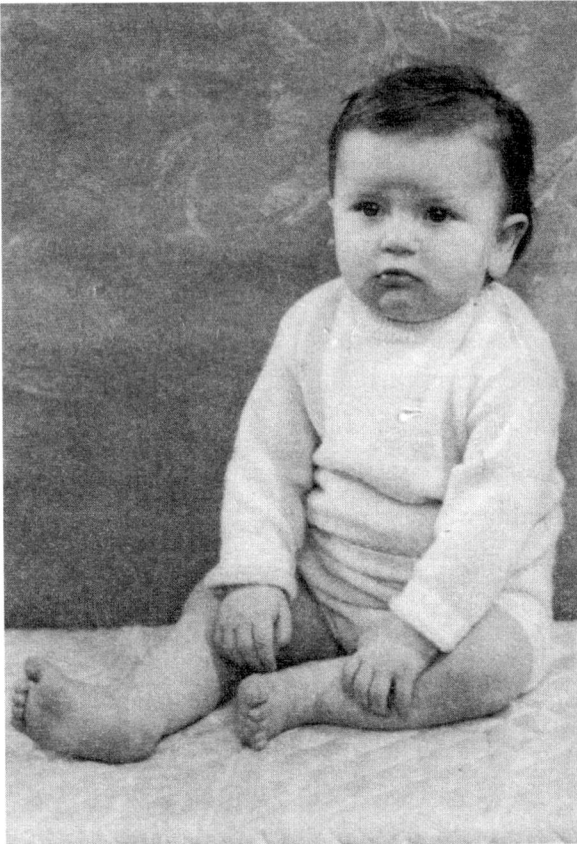

Me as a baby, 1963.

I was the fifth child; the baby and last born of the Joyce siblings. As was expected from an Irish Catholic family at the time, there were a fair few of us – seven, including Mam and Dad. Billy was the eldest, then Martin, then came my two sisters, Bernie and Anne, then, finally, me. Procreation seemed to be my parents' whole *raison d'être*.

My first years were spent in an old Victorian terrace located on Rumford Street, in an area just 2 miles south of Manchester city centre called Chorlton-on-Medlock, or C-on-M as it was known. 'Medlock' was the name of the river that ran through the district. When I say river, I mean in no way an idyllic and pristine stretch of water for swimming and fishing. This river was a cesspool; it had been a source of power during the Industrial Revolution and was eventually condemned as dead due to the amount of industrial waste that flowed into it from the hundreds of factories that lined its banks. If you ever fell into the Medlock, it was straight to the local infirmary for a tetanus shot thanks to the disease-ridden sludge that flowed through it.

As working-class kids, we would spend our time making our own fun, going out and playing in the street. Everything was simpler and there was no sense of anything dangerous lurking outside in the community. That's what was so shocking when the Moors Murders happened between 1963 and 1965 – those poor children. The details of what happened are well known, but the horrific crimes committed by Ian Brady and Myra Hindley absolutely shook the whole nation. I was too young to remember any of it, but it was a much more innocent time. People left their front doors open because nobody had anything, so nobody stole from anybody else. Such was the impact of the murders that Morrissey would later pen the lyrics to 'Suffer Little Children', which mentions the names of the children killed by the demonic couple.

I never encountered overt racism when I was a child, nor indeed at any time growing up in Manchester. During the 1950s and '60s, there had been rampant intolerance directed at Irish immigrants and people of colour. It was not uncommon for boarding houses to have abhorrent signs stating, 'No Irish, No Blacks, No Dogs' displayed in their front windows to discourage those who they felt were unsavoury from stepping over the threshold. Luckily, I never had any sort of this bile to deal with. I think this was because a) I never had an Irish accent; b) although both my parents were immigrants, by the time I was aware of the existence of such hideous discrepancies that may have existed for the older generation, the Irish had assimilated into north of England/British culture in the north west and not brought too much attention to themselves in their daily life; and c) I had white skin so, at first glance, I blended in with those whose lineage went back to beyond the legend of King Arthur. The colour of someone's skin or where they were from really didn't matter to me. Why would it when I was the child of immigrants myself?

My parents, especially my dad, Mick Joyce, however, was often at the sharp end of the then ingrained prejudice. One time, I told Dad that I'd played a gig at a local venue called Band on the Wall, which turned out to be one of his old watering holes.

Dad then proceeded to tell me about how he and a couple of his mates went in there for a pint one lunchtime when they were part of a construction gang on Swan Street. He said a bloke came over to them and said, 'When you Paddies have finished those pints, I want you out.' The plan had been to leave after having just one beer, but with this comment, Mick recalled with a glimmer in his eye, 'Well, after that didn't we all suddenly get a terrible thirst on us!'

The gang stuck around and had a couple more; no one said anything to them. Judging by pictures I've seen of my dad when he was in his prime, I'm not surprised why.

Mick wasn't a particularly tall bloke, but he was strong as an ox. My sister Bernie told me a story from a local church newsletter that was published every week in the village that my dad was from. Local gossip, births, deaths and marriages, that sort of thing. There was a section that included 'thank yous' to people in the community. One read, 'Many thanks to Mick Joyce for catching the bull and bringing it back to the field.' Apparently, this had happened on several occasions when the bull got frisky and would knock down the stone wall to get out of the grazing area in search of some bovine beauties. Now, most folk who have seen a bull – quite sensibly – have viewed it from afar. I get a bit jittery being at close quarters even with a cow because of their size. Well, times its mass by two and its aggression by ten. That's a bull. And my dad single-handedly dragged the beast back to its field. Fearless.

Dad was a navvy when he first came over from Ireland. The term 'navvy' is a shortened form of 'navigator', which referred to general labourers working on railway, road and canal infrastructure across the country from the nineteenth century onwards. The Irish were pretty good at getting stuck into any task. They made for good navvies.

Dad also spent some time working at the gasworks in Manchester. We would often hear stories of him being brought home unconscious in an ambulance after inhaling the fumes. He finally ended up as a coal miner based at the now-defunct Agecroft Colliery. It was a treacherous working environment: 2,500 feet into the dark centre of the earth, old and decrepit equipment unfit for purpose and, on one harrowing occasion, a bloody, grisly scene when a fellow miner lost an arm after it was wrenched clean off by a runaway coal truck.

But his colleagues were not the only victims of the dangers implicit with the job. This was an era when they would take canaries in cages down to the coalface to detect the presence of gas. Such gas in its natural state is odourless. The smell that we today associate with gas is added at a later stage to aid in detecting gas leaks. My dad said that when they had a break for a sandwich, they would look at the bird and will it to perish and fall off the perch. Often a canary would be affected by the gas and sway side to side, its eyes slowly closing. Just as my dad thought he would be freed from a day's labour, the bird would flutter, then stand

9

upright. If this happened, the miners would know there was gas present in the air but that they had to continue regardless. For the miners to go up to ground level, the bird had to fall off the perch. This would signal the end of the working day and the workers would be allowed to go back up, out of the mine.

2

KID OF THE CROFT

We moved just around the corner from Rumford Street to Ackers Street in the mid-'60s. Our building having been erected in the 1800s, the backyard, where the toilet was located, was composed of stone and brick. The short row of houses had previously been used as guest quarters for the stars of the day (including Charlie Chaplin, Gene Vincent, Eddie Cochran and Billy Fury, among others) when they were in Manchester to perform at the nearby Hippodrome on Ardwick Green. By the 1960s, these buildings were dilapidated. There were thousands of such properties in the north west and, as they were council-owned, the cost of regular maintenance was prohibitive.

Just like most kids at the time, we played outside in an area created by old bombed-out buildings from the Second World War that were never rebuilt, amid rows and rows of terraced housing. No grass or trees, just a colourless landscape of crumbling buildings and wasteland – or croft, as it was known. However, we had everything we needed there to spend endless hours entertained.

A rope tied to a lamppost became a swing. When the house next door to ours was demolished, my sister swept the area and built her own 'house' with some of the remaining bricks. It was partitioned too, with a kitchen and living room.

When there was heavy rain, planks of wood pulled from nearby ramshackle homes were adorned with small stones. These would set sail on

Photo of Ackers Street taken by photographer Shirley Baker.
My house is the one along from the end-of-terrace next to the
Holy Name Church in the background of the shot.
© Estate of Shirley Baker / Mary Evans Picture Library

the huge, deep puddles. We would then throw rocks at the 'ships' and knock the stones we'd placed on the planks to 'sink' them. Footballs would be kicked around and passionate matches undertaken. We acquired (stole) some paint from a back yard and painted a start/finish line block across the entrance to Dover Street. Voila! A race circuit that went around the block. I went to a concert at Manchester University about twenty years ago and parked my car on Ackers Street, which is directly opposite the university. I had a look down Dover Street and there it was. It was faint but still marked out in the gutter – our old starting line.

The stationary shells of vehicles – burnt-out, stolen or abandoned cars – became our playground. An ice-cream van was once pilfered by some local hoodlums and ended up parked right outside our house. I don't mean the ice-cream vans that play a merry tune to sell their wares.

I mean a huge lorry that was full of frozen delights that was supposed to be delivered to the local shops. I remember thinking that I'd died and gone to heaven as we prised open the freezer to find it fully stocked with ice cream.

The Holy Name Church was the next building to us on Ackers Street. It was an immense Gothic structure built around the late 1800s, dominating the Manchester skyline. It's still there. In the Joyce family, all activities were centred on or derived from the Catholic Church. Both my mam and dad were staunch Catholics. Mass every Sunday was obligatory.

Every church had a social club attached to it and the social interactions between fellow members of the diocese provided a sense of unity for my parents. The solidarity with the local parishioners was a very important part of life in the Irish community. After all, they were on foreign soil and wanted to be accepted socially.

My mam and dad used to frequent the social club at the Holy Name. The club was the hub of the community. There, decisions were made about what needed to be done in the local area or the church and what needed to happen for any social activities taking place. It also provided the usual entertainment of bingo, Irish-dancing classes, bridge, Easter-bonnet competitions and Whit Walks.*

I won first prize in the Easter-bonnet parade at a church fete there when I was eight. My hat was designed by my sister Bernie who adorned it with a *Saturn V* rocket and a few of the new decimal coins. My prize? A packet of liquorice allsorts, the only sweet in the entire universe that I didn't like.

I became an altar boy when I was about ten years old. The role included such tasks as ringing the altar bell, lighting the candles and preparing the incense, water and wine. As a child, it was a rite of passage,

---

* 'Whit Walks' is shorthand for 'Procession of Witness' – these events were a public expression of faith, with children dressing primarily in white and parading through the streets of Manchester on Whit Friday.

to be associated with the Church and all its accoutrements. If you think about the power of the Church, 800 years ago, and picture the illustrations of the blazing inferno, the Church is telling you, 'This is a depiction of hell.' It's babies on pitchforks. If you show that to people and ask, 'Do you want this? Or do you think you should come to church for a bit of a pray?', they would respond, 'I'll be fucking there like a shot. The whole family, yeah?' That's the vibe of heaven and hell in the Catholic Church. And everyone bought into it.

I'm now a practising atheist (sorry Mam!) as I believe that a lot of Catholic faith is based on fear; certain elements feature the unspoken motto of 'believe ... or else!'

Regardless of my feelings towards religion, at the time I was such a seemingly natural fit for the establishment that I was encouraged to join the priesthood. I even got booked for a visit to a seminary boarding establishment, an educational facility instilling the virtues of the Roman

My First Holy Communion at the Holy Name Church, 1970.

14

KID OF THE CROFT

Catholic faith. In other words, a priests' school. The place frightened me to death with its huge, imposing Victorian stone edifice. The bleakness brought to mind a Thomas Hardy novel; I'd never experienced a place of such austerity.

On entering the building, we came across a number of young lads walking around in pairs for some unknown reason. Each time we passed these boys, they smiled at us in a rather creepy manner. The whole experience felt quite disturbing; it just felt like a place to indoctrinate youths into the Catholic faith, which is exactly what it was. Scary shit. Furthering my religious studies in any formal manner got a hard 'no' from me.

Things were slightly different, though, for my sister Bernie. Her relationship with the Church was a wee bit more intimate. When I was really young, she would invite some of the priests – Father Hackett and Brother Hackett are the ones that I remember – to our house for home-grown renditions of biblical stories, the cast consisting of me and various family members. One memorable outing was our version of 'Jesus lost in the temple'. Our lounge was the temple. My Uncle Martin was about twelve at the time and had been roped into portraying Joseph looking for Jesus. I played Jesus – Jesus hiding under our old upright piano.

'Jesus! Jesus! Where are you?' he cried.

This was my cue to come out and say, 'I'm here, Father!' As I went to get up and reveal my hiding place, I banged my head really hard against the piano. Instead of my required line, I screamed the significantly less devotional line, 'Ow, me fuckin' 'ead!'

There was stunned silence in the room in response to the language that was used by none other than the Son of God. I was only five years old, the youngest in the gang. I'm pretty sure that kind of profane verbiage was used pretty frequently by us all, but not in front of grown-ups – and certainly not in front of the local priests.

X

Victorian neighbourhoods like Ackers Street consisted of rows and rows of terraced housing. The houses were quite big in terms of room size, although I suppose every house would seem large when you're a three-year-old, but you could hear neighbours on both sides. With regard to privacy, everybody knew what everybody's business was. Each room was filled to the brim with chests of drawers and assorted bric-a-brac with massive old wardrobes upstairs. There were pictures on every wall of religious icons and statues, including the Virgin Mary, St Christopher and a multitude of crucifixes on every available surface.

In the 1960s, architects and city officials eventually came around to the idea that such housing was no longer acceptable. They wanted to erect new structures with shops built in and around the actual dwellings. To make room for these 'fabulous' new buildings, the homes of the 1800s had to go. Most, if not all, of these structures were referred to as 'slums' because they were filled with Irish immigrants, the derogatory label slapped on the neighbourhoods inhabited by those considered 'new' to the country. The house on Ackers Street was part of what became known as the 'slum clearance scheme'. I don't know why this was the term used for the housing in this community; it was an offensive label but seemed to go unquestioned. It ended up being one of the biggest clearances of people and houses at the time, all occurring in short order. Huge swathes of these terraces were demolished, with the inhabitants relocated in supposedly improved accommodation. Things were changing. The council believed that concrete dwellings in the sky were the way forward for the people of Manchester, as was the case across the rest of the country. Well, the majority of this new housing built in the 1960s and widely touted as being a kind of 'paradise' was so badly constructed that it was flattened in the 2010s and rebuilt yet again. Like the modernist structures of its bright mid-century future, Ackers Street and its sprawling community of old Victorian houses is now long gone.

3

OUR LORD

Just before our place on Ackers Street was flattened in the slum clearance, my dad was given three options for relocation, all within the greater Manchester area.

Wythenshawe: a huge modern housing estate that was to be the largest in Europe; Ancoats: an area adjacent to Manchester city centre; or Fallowfield: another gargantuan housing estate in south Manchester's suburbs. On the face of it, I had no idea what these places were like. As a seven-year-old, I'd never been to any of them. I accompanied my dad to view the house in Fallowfield. I think he decided to check that particular location out first as it would have been the easiest to get to from where we currently lived just south of the centre.

We got on the number 48 bus from Oxford Road to look at our potential new abode. The first thing I noticed was that Wilbraham Road seemed so green. Trees lined both sides of the road. I felt like I'd arrived in a foreign country. The furthest I'd been with my parents at that age was the annual one-week holiday to every northern working-class family's summer vacation: Blackpool. The obvious attraction of Blackpool was the fact that it was a seaside town. Fallowfield was not. But compared to Ackers Street, it looked so lush and had so many wide-open spaces. The houses even had spaces between them! Semi-detached living was still an impressive novelty to this former terrace dweller. And the road looked huge – a dual carriageway complete with grassy central reservation. I was impressed.

The new place at 181 Wilbraham Road was a major step up from our last house. Being of Edwardian build, it only shared one wall with one other building for starters. It even had an inside toilet. There was a front garden with a small ornamental tree in the centre of the lawn that had the most beautiful, vibrant yellow, pendulous flowers. I later found out it was called a laburnum. We even had a back garden too. I think this is what the council hoped would make people's lives a little bit more tranquil and a little less, well, *brick and stone.*

To the rear of the house were fields that featured a small pig farm. That meant there was plenty of opportunity for adventure, something to fill the void that had been created since leaving Ackers Street.

Dad didn't even bother going to see the other two places on offer. I was now a Fallowfield lad.

In Fallowfield, most of the people were Irish. It must have been a conscious decision for the council to put them into areas where there would be a strong community, where they wouldn't feel left out or scared. A friend of mine, of Pakistani origin, told me a similar story. He said that when his dad emigrated to Manchester, he lived in a house with about eight or ten other guys from Pakistan. If one of them had been assigned to live in a housing estate on their own, it would have been terrifying, not to mention an insane culture shock; that's why the council put them all together. I think that's what they did with the Irish as well.

Around this time, I became aware of 'class'. All the housing on the estate was council-owned in the 1970s. My next-door neighbours were the exception; they had somehow managed to buy their place. The Housing Act of 1980 introduced the Right to Buy scheme in the UK, granting eligible council tenants the right to purchase their homes at a discounted price. But in the first half of the '70s, it was almost unheard of in our neighbourhood for someone to actually be on the housing ladder in their own right.

Me, Mam and the cat at Wilbraham Road, 1973.

All the government-owned properties had the same windows and doors; you couldn't change them as the council owned them. But if *you* owned the house, you could do what the hell you wanted with them. Well, our neighbours changed the gate, the doors *and* the windows. It was definitely a way to show the outside world that they were of a different, *better* 'class' than those around them.

These contrasts were even evident in the food that we ate. I clearly remember seeing one of the kids from next door tucking into chicken sandwiches. I thought he was a cut above the rest of us. In our house, the food almost never deviated from meat and cabbage. And if it did, it only did so for the usual fine delicacies of meat and potato pie and chips from the local chippy.

It was only once we had moved that we noticed that the area didn't have a social club. So what did my dad do? He got together with all the other Irish navvies and built one from scratch. It's still there now and it's still open as a social club. At the weekends, it would be absolutely packed for dance nights; you couldn't move in there.

There was a committee at the club. They talked about what needed to be done in the local area, what needed to be done for the church and what social activities were appealing, whether it be Gaelic football, hurling or other traditional Irish sports. A committee of about eight men – always men – would make executive decisions between them. Every weekend, they would all meet up and discuss business. They'd talk, work, imbibe a few drinks and then later on they would have a dance to Irish bands, such as Aiden and the Strangers or Big Tom and the Mainliners.

All the adults that I knew from the area went there. I thought that was what everybody in the world did every weekend, in their own local club, wherever it was. It's something that I took for granted – all the adults across the country having a dance on a Saturday night.

One day, I was talking to an English kid called Wayne Bradley about our weekend plans. I was telling him how all our parents went out dancing. He was completely shocked that adults would exhibit *that kind* of behaviour. 'What do you mean, *dancing?*', he asked suspiciously. I was taken aback that he thought it was weird.

Wayne Bradley, however, was stunned.

Wayne was a Protestant, though religious differences rarely came up. One day, we were playing snooker on a small-sized table I had set up in my room. We had saintly statues all around the house: Mary and Joseph, Jesus on the cross. My domain was not exempt from the holy décor, as nailed to the wall was a picture of the Sacred Heart. It's the famous image of Jesus with his arms outstretched. He was dressed in a robe, opened in the front to reveal his gold, glowing heart.

As Wayne lined up his shot, he hit the Jesus picture with the end of his snooker cue. I was immediately engulfed by a cold wave of horror, not for fear of being struck down by the Almighty, but by the terror of the battering that I would receive from my mam and dad if the stick went through the framed relic. I waved my hands urgently in the air, in front of Wayne's face, frantically screeching, 'Watch our Lord!'

Wayne stopped, put down the cue and looked me up and down. 'He's my Lord as well,' he proclaimed. Not wanting to start a fight, I decided to double down, in an attempt to explain my choice of words. 'No,' I slowly replied, 'I didn't mean he is OUR LORD as in the Catholics have sole ownership and not the Protestants. He's *your* Lord, too.' I paused to further ponder proprietorship of the deity. 'He's *everybody's* Lord, I think,' I concluded, in an attempt to be diplomatic to my guest. Once both sides of the religious divide had settled their differences over the confusion of whose 'Lord' it was, we got back to our snooker game.

Although there was tension between the English Protestants and the Irish Catholics, it didn't bother me. Then, as now, I wasn't interested in profiling somebody because of their religious denomination, their colour or where they were from in the world.

I did not know the other Smiths until we were in a band together, yet we were almost immediately a close-knit group. We found out later that we were all the product of Irish Catholic, immigrant, working-class parents, which no doubt provided a subconscious foundation of understanding. Unlike my Protestant friend Wayne, the other three lads in the band recognised exactly where I came from, the values instilled without a word having to be exchanged and the parental wrath incurred at ramming a snooker cue through the chest of our Lord.

4

SOCIAL MEAT

When relatives from Ireland would come to visit us in Manchester, they would more often than not experience an extreme culture clash. England offered a very different lifestyle. On one occasion, one of my cousins took her very first flight to see us. Arriving at Manchester Airport and desperate for a wee, she rushed into the nearest toilets only to be faced with a strange ceramic bowl attached to the wall. Gripping the pipe running up the back of the outlet for dear life, she had her knickers down, awkwardly half-squatting over the urinal when a male traveller entered the gents and had quite a surprise... and the penny dropped. It was all bizarre and new.

My mam had a similar cultural collision several years later. When the Smiths played in London at the prestigious Royal Albert Hall, I convinced her and Auntie Nan to come and see us perform. They'd never been on a plane before either, so I flew them down from Manchester and booked them in at the very swish Hyde Park Hotel. I made sure that there was champagne and flowers waiting for them on arrival. I wanted them to be spoiled, for them to cut loose and have a good time. I made sure that I was there when they checked in and showed them to their room. They seemed a bit overwhelmed by it all, but I told them to take it easy and that I'd pop by in an hour or two to make sure that they were okay.

However, on my return, I found a sobering scene. They were both sitting stiffly on the bed, still in their coats. They felt so alien in this beautiful space. I encouraged them to go and explore, have a look around the shops. Mam said, 'No, I think we'll be alright here.' More animatedly, my auntie had an idea. 'Are there any bookmakers nearby?' she asked. It was the first excitement I had witnessed all day from either of them. With a sigh, I decided to leave them to it, hoping that they would crack into the fizz and start to unwind. Yet when I came back later, they still hadn't moved. They'd never been inside a place this opulent before and found it difficult to relax. The champagne remained unopened.

My dad used to go back to the homeland every summer without fail to help his brother in the fields during harvest time. I joined him once when I was about nine. He held my hand as we rushed through the railway station, him shouting at a fella, 'Hey John, what platform is the Galway train leaving from?' I did not know that referring to a stranger as 'John' in Ireland was the same as saying, 'Hey mate' in England. I thought my dad was so cool as not only did he know everything, but he also knew everybody too, and by their first names, no less.

On walking into the Joyce homestead in Ireland, there was much enthusiastic greeting. We sat down for tea and I was given a plate of meat and potatoes. The potatoes were served in what I can only describe as a barrel with handles. Plenty of butter was mixed in with the spuds. When I dived in for a first bite, I was astounded. 'Wow, Dad, what kind of potatoes are these? They're the best I've ever had!' Much laughter filled the room. 'They're OUR potatoes, Michael.'*

After we finished eating, my dad caught up on all the local news with Uncle Bill. At bedtime, the whole family entered the large kitchen and knelt down on the stone floor; I had no clue what was happening. Rosary beads appeared in hands and Aunty Mary started to recite what

---

* The next time I had a similar experience was fifty years later when I harvested my first spuds from the allotment, which I've had for ten years now. What do I use to feed mine? Just rainwater and sunshine, just like my Uncle Bill in Ireland; those are the not so 'secret ingredients' that make a fabulous-tasting potato.

I recognised as 'The Lord's Prayer'. She stopped halfway through at the 'On earth as it is in heaven' part and, without missing a beat, the whole family (with the exception of me) replied in unison with the latter part of the benediction.

The same happened with the 'Hail Mary' and 'Glory Be' devotions. For those who aren't familiar with rosary beads, each bead represents a prayer and they're in ten lots of ten bead sections for the Hail Marys and two slightly different beads for the Our Father and Glory Be prayers. The recital of the rosary lasted about twenty minutes as every bead was covered. I knew my mam and dad held strong Catholic beliefs, but this was on another level.

It wasn't just potatoes that we grew on the homestead. There were dairy cows that needed tending to and all hands were on deck in the two weeks in August to build up the haystacks for the winter.

I helped my cousins and the farmhands carry the containers of milk down to the fields for the grown-ups. When there was a break for lunch, my dad asked me if I wanted a swig of milk. I looked inside the billy can and, after seeing the contents, decided I was not that thirsty after all. This wasn't milk as I knew it; it was thick and creamy and with a yellowish hue.

'It's delicious,' my dad reassured me. 'It came straight from the teat this morning.' I took his word for it but declined. My idea of delicious milk and his were obviously very different – I liked mine straight from the fridge, not the udder.

My dad was obsessed with cuts of meat, the fatter the better. In retrospect, it showed a mind-blowing lack of understanding of how to manage a balanced diet. How would he know any different though? Food was regarded as sustenance, the inherent dangers of calorific content, carbs, salt intake or fatty steaks dripping with tallow and other cholesterol-rich food were a complete mystery to my ol' fella and everyone in his household.

Many years later, in about 1985, I picked him up from Manchester Airport after he came back from Ireland. When I took his suitcase off the trolley, I could hardly lift it.

'What on earth have you got in there, Dad?!' I grunted. It felt like it was full of bricks.

When we got back to his house, we managed to get the case inside. I was dying to see what mysteries it contained. When he revealed the contents, there was something wrapped in a black bin liner on the top of his clothes. He picked it up with great difficulty and threw it over his shoulder. The way he had to manoeuvre this great bulk made it look like he had shipped back a dead body. He took it into the kitchen, got a huge knife out and split the bag from the top to the bottom. He peeled back the plastic. Inside was a carcass.

The outside still had hair, and he turned it over to reveal a pink interior.

'Well, would you look at that!' he announced proudly. 'A lovely cut of meat!'

I couldn't believe what I was seeing. 'You've brought a dead *pig* home in your suitcase, Dad?', I gasped incredulously.

Of course, he didn't think anything of it.

'Arah, what harm?' was his reply.

He put a huge 'S' hook into the top of it, stripped off the bin bag and hung it up in a large cupboard in the kitchen. It had been salted to stop it from rotting. He had it dangling in there for months, taking a cut from it each day. And for those of you keeping track of dates, yes, we had released *Meat is Murder* earlier that year, and yes, I had been a vegetarian since we started recording the album. I was merely shocked. Morrissey would have been horrified.

But this was my dad and I would forgive him most things – a strong, proud and much-loved 'Mayo man'. Being of a certain generation, he rarely showed any affection to me or my other brothers and sisters, but I didn't feel he needed to. I have nothing but great memories of him.

5

SMELLS LIKE FRUIT

Being the youngest of five children, I was the spoilt 'baby' of the family. A life-changing event when I was nine would only further entrench this view.

One night, my dad asked me to get some coal for the fire from the storage in the back garden. We received a regular allowance of coal as part of his pay for working in the mine. I went outside with a shovel and a small bucket to undertake the chore. When I opened the back door, it was snowing. Oh yeah! Forget the coal. I'm going out front to play. I put a coat on and went out the front door to see the flakes cascading down, glittering under the sodium-yellow street lighting on Wilbraham Road.

That is the last thing I remember.

Coming home from work later that evening, my mam entered the road to be greeted by the urgent bustle of the emergency services disturbing the peaceful calm of the falling snow. There were ambulances and police everywhere.

She spoke to one of our neighbours who told her that a young girl had been badly injured in a car crash just outside our house.

But it wasn't a girl at all; it was me. Mam fainted and was taken inside. There was quite a lot of blood from the impact of my head striking the rocks under our hedge. The contrast of that red claret against the white snow made for a shocking and rather grisly tableau.

It was bad. Really bad. My parents and siblings were all told to prepare for the very real possibility that I might die. On arrival at the hospital, a priest was brought to my bedside to administer the last rites, ensuring my soul a smooth transition to the next life, just in case the worst prognosis came to be and I failed to regain consciousness.

It won't surprise you to learn that I pulled through. And, early the next morning, I came to, surrounded by my family in an unfamiliar bright room. I was no longer outside playing in the snow. I was extremely confused.

They didn't go into too much detail – I was still in recovery – but I later found out that a van lost control on the snow, careered off the road and onto the pavement. It first hit the caretaker from the local primary school, a Mr Finn, sending him over the topiary in front of our house. He had been innocently strolling down the street when the vehicle struck him from behind, throwing him 30 feet into the air, before smashing his head on the door frame of a nearby house. He survived, but I have no idea how. His blood was still spattered across the neighbour's house when I was eventually released from hospital, having yet to be mopped up.

After disposing of Mr Finn, the van continued its diabolical trajectory, smashing directly into yours truly before pushing me face first into the bushes at the front of our garden, splitting my head open on collision with the hard surface beneath. It took no fewer than thirty stitches to put me back together. My collarbone was instantly broken on impact. And yet neither of these injuries were responsible for the summoning of the priest. That was down to my spleen.

I had a very brief and strange moment of clarity when I arrived at the hospital. I woke up and told the nurse sitting beside my bed that she 'owed me £50'. She asked what I meant by this and I told her that it was because 'she'd landed on Pall Mall'. At the same time, I was able to briefly tell her about an awful pain in my stomach before I slipped back into oblivion.

In my delirium, and clearly still enamoured with the Monopoly set I had been bought for Christmas, it had become *crucial* that I collect what I thought I was owed for rent on a house I owned on the coveted Pall Mall. While she didn't hand over the cash, the nurse did take my moment of lucid agony seriously and summoned a doctor who immediately recommended exploratory surgery.

When I was opened up, it was discovered that I was bleeding to death internally from a ruptured spleen. It had been damaged when the van had hit my side. Although I was x-rayed immediately on arrival at the hospital to gauge the extent of my injuries, that particular trauma had not shown up. If I hadn't woken up for that sixty-second moment when I spoke to the nurse, they reckoned I wouldn't have survived.

I was in hospital for six months.

The staff were lovely but brisk. Everything was very clean and white; the sister on the ward made sure of that. She would look in the corners and wipe a cloth or finger over every nook and cranny of the rooms, on the prowl for dust like an obsessed hotel inspector. The consultants were considered gods; no questions were to be asked as they were always right. It was always 'Doctor' not 'the doctor'. There was an air of formality among the staff. The only occasion I remember seeing anyone in scrubs was when they were on their way to the theatre for a procedure. The rest of the time, the nurses wore dresses accessorised by little watches dangling from a strap pinned to their lapels. Doctors were always in shirts and ties, adding a white lab coat sporadically for a touch of flair.

Because my injuries were so severe, I had been placed initially into the main wing with the adults instead of being bundled into the children's ward.

Entertainment and distraction were non-existent. It was relentless boredom; difficult for anybody when convalescing in a hospital, but for one so young, a living nightmare. There were no toys, no books, nothing to take my mind off being stuck in a bed surrounded by adult men in various states of illness. The only reprieve offered was one 14-inch black-and-white television for the entire wing, located in a day room, which was usually inhabited with men watching the horse racing and chain smoking. The walls there were yellow with tar and nicotine, the one area not under Sister's cleanliness regime.

I had plenty of visits, but from family only and just during specific restricted hours. Parents were not allowed to stay overnight; it could be very scary as I was often on my own, being too young to have friends come by.

Anything that broke up the days of waiting to see my family and staring at a wall were memorable as so little happened. My brother Martin tried to alleviate the monotony, bringing me a plastic Airfix model of a Sunderland flying boat that I could build myself to help me pass the time. However, it was too complicated for me and, for the rest of my stay, it sat tantalisingly close in its box on my bedside table, taunting me with the possibility of completion.

At one point, I was put on a glucose drip and allowed just small sips of water. 'Nil by mouth', I think is the technical term. Shortly after my mam came to visit, armed with the traditional glass bottle of Lucozade in crispy gold cellophane and a huge bunch of grapes in a slightly less presentable paper bag. I wasn't strictly allowed either. But my mam was undeterred.

'Go on, just a have a few grapes. They can't do you that much harm.'

I grabbed a handful and rammed them all in my mouth. I started devouring them. Oh heaven!

Shortly after, the nurse entered the room.

She quickly spied the bag of grapes on my bedside table.

'You've not eaten any of those, have you?', she interrogated.

I look at Mam, Mam looks at the nurse, the nurse looks at me. It was a Mexican standoff in the infirmary. Who's going to make the first move? Itchy trigger fingers were quickly discarded for caringly insistent but surgically gloved hands. It was so bloody obvious that I had eaten some of the grapes.

'Well, we'll have to get rid of *those!*' the nurse proclaimed.

I felt a mixture of fear and confusion. How the hell is she going to do that?! She pulled the curtain around the bed and took off the dressing covering my stomach area.

There was a small plastic tube attached to my left side, about a centimetre in width and 2 to 3 centimetres in length. She inserted a hypodermic syringe into the tube and drew it up. She did this quite a few times with increasing pressure and determination, finally getting the result she needed.

And as I looked down, to my horror, the skins of the grapes started to appear, slurping their way up the tube with every plunge of the syringe.

From that point on, I did as I was told.

X

I was absolutely delighted when I finally went home. The hospital stay had been a miserable experience.

On entering the house, the first thing I noticed was a huge new television in the corner of the room. I had been carried into the house and was delicately plonked on the couch opposite this new wonder. This was to be my bed while recuperating.

The very first time I experienced a seizure I was watching the TV. It was about 10 feet away from me, in the corner of the room. Suddenly, I noticed the TV seeming to jump towards me; before long it was mere inches from my face. Then, in one swift movement, it was back in the corner. Before I could catch my breath, the same thing happened again; the TV got very close to my face, then retreated. This repeated itself over and over, getting progressively quicker each time. Far ... near ... far ... near, faster and faster. I blacked out.

When I came round, my sisters and mam were standing over me sobbing. 'What's wrong?', I asked. All they could do in reply was sob. I was completely unaware that I'd had an epileptic fit, but they had witnessed the whole episode.

Back to the hospital I went, where I was given an electroencephalogram examination (EEG). I had numerous tests with specialists where they placed what looked like a rubber cycling helmet on my head and attached wires to it to check brain activity. A strobe was then placed directly in front of my face, while doctors examined the readings. It was a thoroughly unpleasant experience. After the full battery of grim procedures, I was officially diagnosed with epilepsy.

I've since been in the presence of somebody who has had an epileptic fit and found the experience absolutely terrifying. In hindsight, I completely understand why my family were so upset at seeing me convulsing, especially considering I was only a child at the time.

I had a few more of these attacks and they would always begin the same way. I would be looking at an object then, without warning, it would be right in front of my face. The tempo would quicken until I lost consciousness.

I was eventually prescribed Phenobarbital. I had a number of other fits over the next year. Strangely, they just stopped as suddenly as they had started. The general consensus was that the epilepsy was brought on by the accident. Luckily for me, I've never experienced another episode, but as the accident was deemed responsible, my family were able to make an insurance claim. We were successful in the claim and a few thousand pounds was put into a trust for me that couldn't be accessed until I was sixteen. This money came in quite handy when I moved out of the family home.

So, the spoilt baby of the family was now the super, precious and *ridiculously* spoilt baby of the family who had nearly lost his life. I could've asked my mum for the moon and she would have asked me, 'Which one? Full? Crescent? Half?'

6

A CRACK ON THE HEAD

I was told by Mam that my school had been in touch with regard to my 11+ exam that I was due to take early the next year. The results of my tests would determine what type of education I would be offered next: a grammar school place or secondary modern. Grammar schools were generally considered to be an educational facility with a more academic curriculum, seeing a significant proportion of the pupils progressing to university. Secondary modern schools concentrated more on practical subjects. Passing the 11+ was viewed as key in laying the foundation for a financially buoyant adult life. Because I'd missed so much of my schooling (about twelve months) due to the accident, it was advised that I stay on another year to catch up on all I'd missed so as to not fail the vital test and thus doom myself to a life of – gasp! – practical skilled labour.

There was no way I was going to let this happen. Stay another year in junior school – baby school! – while all my mates went to secondary? No chance. Filled with the bravado that only one who has had a brush with death can muster, I took the exam against everyone's better judgement. And passed it.

It was 1974 when I turned eleven and entered St Gregory's Grammar School in Ardwick, Manchester. Although there were some younger teachers, an 'older' brigade in their forties and fifties loomed over the faculty. Some of these guys were born in the 1920s and '30s, and they had brought their archaic disciplinary practices with them. Corporal punishment in

Manchester schools was standard practice. And some of this lot were truly sadistic in nature.

In my first year, during chemistry, I was speaking to the lad next to me when I suddenly felt a sharp pain on the back of my head. I momentarily blacked out. When I lifted my face off the desk, the teacher was screaming at me to pay attention in class. The lad behind me said the teacher had been at the back of the room, saw me speaking, sneaked up behind me and rapped the back of my head with his clenched fist. He meted out this punishment/assault on an eleven-year-old child. The result was a huge lump on the top of my sore head. Belligerent ghouls *did* run Manchester schools.

That night at home, I had an epileptic fit. This was totally unexpected as I'd been fit-free for more than a year. I mentioned to my mam that it may have been brought on by the punch to the nut I'd received. She was furious. She said that she would be going in to school first thing in the morning to have it out with the headmaster and teacher concerned. I begged her not to as I was afraid my card would be marked if she did. Mam said that she didn't mind me receiving any type of corporal punishment whether it be slipper, strap or cane – but a blow to the head, for medical reasons, was just too much!

The next day, we had a meeting with the headmaster and teacher who administered the blow. My mam told them what she'd said to me about receiving further punishments. They both agreed that if there was to be any future action taken in the form of discipline, it would have to be the other forms discussed, not a punch to the noggin given my medical history. And for that I think I was meant to be grateful...

Corporal punishment was viewed by many as the main tool to correct behaviour deemed undesirable. Any minor infraction judged to be out of line could result in a run in with violence. But, of course, the threat of physical pain did not foster a positive attitude towards learning or being in the classroom. If anything, it made authority figures like educators seem like demonic entities out to harm for their own malicious pleasure.

One day, our regular teacher was absent. We had a substitute who was obviously pissed off about being drafted in to look after us for thirty minutes. He really would rather have been in the staff room, smoking a cigarette, scanning the upcoming horse races in the newspaper and drinking tea.

He told us to be quiet.

At first, it went silent. Then people started talking to each other.

He told everyone to shut up.

We did, but then the talking gradually began again.

Suddenly, he stood up.

'Right, that's it, I've had enough!' he bellowed.

He took a strap* out of the inside pocket of his sport jacket where he had it conveniently stored for easy access, as one would any accoutrement in regular usage. He began rapping the strap against his thigh, making a dreadful slapping sound, openly relishing the now palpable trepidation emanating from every student in the room. The sickening, almost wet crack of the strap confirmed that any contact with the punishment device was going to be terribly painful.

The sub told the lad at the front of the class to hold out his hand before administering three blows to the outstretched appendage. The poor lad winced in agony. He then ordered the chap next to him to stand up and do the same. Another three blows. Then the next row.

There were thirty-five kids in this class, so it was some undertaking. By the time the substitute teacher had finished the first row, he walked back to the front of the class and removed his jacket, revealing an exhibition of sweat spreading across his back, chest and under the arms.

---

* For those unfamiliar with the physiology of this torture device, a strap is a piece of leather about 20 centimetres in length and around 5 centimetres in width, with the end split into three strands for inflicting maximum pain.

I'll never forget the look on his face as he was carrying out this punishment: a crimson grimace of venomous delight from the strain of beating a roomful of children. He was completely bloody deranged. God, I hated that place.

By the time I reached my third year, I had started to really resent it. The menacing atmosphere of teachers made it an unpleasant and feared place to be. Rather than be cajoled or encouraged to get back on board with my learning, my disengagement – when it was noticed at all – was met with brutality.

On the plus side, there was a lad in my year called John Fox. We got on really well. He was from Longsight, a neighbourhood in Manchester that was only a couple of miles from where I lived in Fallowfield. His parents were also immigrants from Ireland, hailing from Dublin. We hung out with each other all the time and became best friends. This friendship would last way beyond my school years and into adulthood. Over the years, we would go and watch Manchester City together and our musical tastes were virtually identical. We frequented many gigs in Manchester and beyond. 'Foxy' was my best man at my wedding.

7

MR ROMANTIC

At twelve, I'd started going to the local dance night at St Kentigern's Social Club. The social club was part of the church, an important component of the Irish network for kids and grown-ups alike.

The age range was, supposedly, a strict thirteen- to seventeen-year-olds; no adults were allowed in, nor very young children. I was well under the minimum age, but because my mum and dad were well-connected in that circle, I was granted admission.

It was all very exciting. There were lads bringing in beers, sneaking them in through the toilets. One of the older-looking boys would go into a nearby off-licence to get a bottle of cider, furtively smuggle it through the doors before distilling the lukewarm liquid into a little plastic cup that'd be shared around between everybody. A tiny sip of cider for a kid who was not even a teenager seemed quite dangerous.

I was by far the youngest of the St Kent's gang. They were all in their teens, but the difference between a sixteen-year-old and a twelve-year-old is profound. I used to walk in and see all these lads with the girls and think, *This is where it's at. I'm with grown-ups now. Maybe* I'm *a cool dude?*

As with the adults, music played a big part in social activities. All the lads stood in a row for the dance routine they'd worked out for 'Gerdundula' by Status Quo, with its Irish/Celtic lilt. It didn't look that difficult to pull off. Right foot crossing the left, left foot back, right foot back. Left foot forward, right crossing the left again and repeat. I never dared to try though as there was a hierarchy as to who was allowed to join the line-up. Because of the age difference, I would never have attempted to join in with the 'big lads'.

I received my first snog in St Kent's from one of the local girls in our gang. An outing to the local chip shop was undertaken afterwards in celebration of this momentous – for me, still twelve – achievement. The night was very cold and we were in the doorway of the takeaway. She had her arms around me, cuddling up under the guise of wanting to keep warm. She was about fifteen or sixteen and I was younger. I would never have come on to a girl like that because I was still a child with no idea of what to do. We never went out with each other; it was a one-night affair, but it was my greatest accomplishment to date. I went back to the house like Billy Big Bollocks. I thought I was Mr Romantic, kissing girls and sipping a clandestine cup of cider. I've arrived. I am the geezer.

At the time, my mam worked in the cloakroom at St Kent's on weekends. I would sit behind her, helping keep everything organised in the manic rushes that invariably occurred at the start and end of the evenings. Not quite the lad-about-town geezer after all. It was two pence to put your coat in there with us for the night. Later, I worked there as a pot collector, going around getting all the glasses, sorting them out, throwing the bottles in the skip, recycling broken glasses and washing the rest.

With my sister Anne being the closest to me in age, I felt that I had more of an affinity with her than my much older brothers and sister. My two elder brothers, Martin and Billy, had long flown the nest. So 'our kid' kind of took me under her wing. Anne was a bit of a bad girl. She would have been sixteen when I was twelve.

We lived close to Manchester City's ground in Fallowfield; you could hear the roar of the crowd from our house. Anne would take me to Maine Road with all her mates who were Blues, a crew known affectionately as MCFC Boot Girls. Anne was quite a tough kid. She was hard and her mates were hard. They used to go down and 'welcome' opposition

The Joyces around 1975 – Anne is second from the left.

fans who came to Maine Road to watch City. There was more than an undercurrent of violence. A lot of the kids would carry metal combs with handles that had been sharpened to blades. Yeah, it was pretty tough.

There was a strong element of tribalism that ran through the whole scene. In Manchester, in the '70s, you wanted to be part of *some* scene, whatever that was. You were recognised by the clothes you wore, which would give an indication of what music you were into and which football team you supported. Music, fashion and football: an important combination of every discernible youth culture when we were coming of age.

When Mam and Dad went to the club and left us at home, Anne would bust out her record collection, inviting some of the local lads and girls to come over and participate in the unchaperoned revelry. Anne knew she couldn't get rid of me, so a sneaky glass of cider and the odd cigarette always helped to keep my mouth shut.

There were always a couple of scooters parked outside on the pavement during these parties and I was always impressed with how cool the lads were that she was hanging out with.

Music was a language, a means of having a conversation without a word being spoken. The records were the medium. Disco, rock and plenty of ska were in the mix. Judge Dread was the artist of choice. I wasn't a huge fan of the music that Anne listened to back then; I was a bit too young to appreciate just how good it was. And this was 1975, pre-punk, so 'Get Dancin'' by Disco-Tex and the Sex-O-Lettes, Hot Chocolate's 'You Sexy Thing' and 'The Hustle' by Van McCoy were all personal favourites.

In an attempt to help make me cool, Anne took me to a shop in Manchester called Stolen From Ivor, located in the Underground Market near where the Arndale Centre is now. She was a 'suedehead' and wanted to dress up her little brother in the same fashion. Being a 'suedehead' meant embracing a very definite style of dress, a very singular look that quickly associated you with that particular subculture. Anne bought me a green two-tone suit, a Trutex button-down shirt and a Crombie coat – a staple for anyone in that scene. Mine was navy blue with a little red handkerchief coming out of the top pocket. I had checked trousers, a pair of brogues and red socks matching the handkerchief. I even had my hair cut short. It was a strong look, especially for someone barely out of junior school.

There were a couple of crews, or 'mobs' as they were known, made up of the kids that lived in the local area. The Netherton Mob, the Thelwall Mob, the Rostherne Mob and us lot, the Fallowfield Mob. I was the young-est in the Fallowfield Mob, with most of my mates being two or three years older than me. It doesn't sound like a lot, but when you're thirteen, a sixteen-year-old is an old and wise master.

You didn't want to walk through these neighbourhoods if you were from a different mob. If you accidentally stepped foot in another group's territory, you could be the recipient of a good hiding. Mind you, the differences in the demarked dominions of each of these crews was a matter of a few hundred yards or so; you could walk fewer than two minutes from your own house and suddenly be in an enemy enclave. The names of these gangs – 'Thelwall', 'Netherton' and 'Rostherne' – were named after the roads where they were based. And if you did find yourself inadvertently trespassing, the scenario played out with regimented familiarity. Firstly, a couple of lads from the rival mob would whistle or shout to catch your attention. Nothing overly threatening but an early warning shot. This would be followed by a beckoning or slightly more confrontational 'Oi!' being yelled in your direction. At this point, you would find yourself being edged towards a more unfamiliar street or – worse still – a cul-de-sac by your would-be assailants. Before long, you'd realise it was too late. They'd set the trap and drawn you in and you'd suddenly have twenty lads charging you down. At this point, you had two choices. Stand your ground – don't be a fool! – or run like hell.

There were no knives or guns then; it was all fists, but those could do some serious damage. I know it sounds pretty dramatic, but it was the kind of thing that was happening in just about every area in Manchester. It wasn't a daily occurrence, though, just something that you had to be aware of and prepared for.

Several years later, when I was seventeen, I found myself on Adelphi Street in Salford. I'd been to Pips Disco in Manchester with my mates Ade, Grinner and Jackie, his girlfriend at the time. Pips was a great place to hang out for kids who were into Bowie, Roxy Music, punk and alternative artists. It was a big club, but most of my friends used to go straight to the 'Roxy Room'. There was no dress code, though a lot of the clientele would really make the effort to be as outlandishly turned out as possible. They used to have gigs too. Joy Division played their debut headline show there as Warsaw in 1978. Unfortunately, I wasn't there. The only gig I saw there was Spizzenergi.

As we got ready to leave Pips, we were invited to a party in a block of flats out west in Salford. When we went into the lounge, there were about five or six lads sitting in a circle on the floor with their heads in a black bin bag that had been filled with glue or some other type of solvent. We decided it wasn't our kind of scene and split.

When we got out of the lift at the bottom of the high-rise flats, a couple of boys were shouting at us and taking the piss. We couldn't make out exactly what they were saying, but it certainly wasn't 'Welcome to Salford!' They looked like young teenagers, about thirteen years old or so. We shouted back and told them to go fuck themselves. As they carried on screaming abuse at us, we turned away to go home. When they saw us leaving, they ran towards us roaring, 'Come on, you fucking cowards. Let's have it!' Because they were so young, we weren't taking the bait and ignored them. They ran at us again shouting, 'Come on!'

At this point, my mate Ade took off his belt and said to me and Grinner, 'I've had enough of this. Let's teach them a lesson, the cheeky bastards.' I really didn't see the point, but we had to back up our mate Ade. We gave chase and they ran off down a little side street. They appeared again, but this time behind us. 'Over 'ere lads!' We ran after them again down the road and into another street then ... Bang!

About two dozen blokes just appeared out of nowhere. They were running towards us brandishing sticks and bats, chucking bricks at us. I know that if you're on somebody else's turf, you usually keep your head down, but their baiting tactic was on another level. It was almost impressive. There's always been an underlying rivalry between the two cities of Manchester and Salford, going back hundreds of years, but I had never experienced it first-hand. Until now.

We got split up in the commotion and me, Ade and Jackie got a good leathering. Then something pretty weird happened. One of the older kids flagged down a black cab that was passing and put us in it; we were already a bit battered and bruised. He said, 'Don't ever come round 'ere again, this is Salford.' The three of us took the ride. However, Grinner was nowhere to be seen, having got separated from us in the melee. We later found out he was in Hope Hospital, having the bottom half of his ear stitched back on after being hit on the side of his face by one of the bricks that had been raining down on us.

The next day, following his treatment at the local infirmary, we were interviewed by the Salford police. We were shown a catalogue of mug shots and asked if we recognised any of the assailants from the attack in the Bumper Book of Crims. I immediately saw three of the boys, as well as the one who put us in the cab. With a scar running diagonally across his face from his right eyebrow to his lower left jaw, he was hard to forget.

'Nope, no one looks familiar,' I said.

'Are you sure?'

'Yep, no one,' I replied. The police then had another idea.

'We know who this lot are. They hang out around the chippy at the bottom of the high-rise block of flats. Let's go down there now and you can point them out.'

Yeah, right! You've got two chances of me doing that: 'no chance' and 'fat chance'. I would have loved nothing more than to go down where these lads hung out in a police car and say, 'Yes, constable, it was him and him and that one there.' But that was *never* gonna happen. From then on, we just gave Salford a wide berth on our night-time adventures.

8

EVER FALLEN IN LOVE

1977-1978

Buzzcocks were becoming huge in Manchester music circles. They were the first punk band in the UK to release an independent punk record – *Spiral Scratch* – on their label New Hormones. Original lead singer Howard Devoto left not long after *Spiral Scratch* was released, seeing bandmate Pete Shelley take over on frontman duties. Both of them had put on the legendary Sex Pistols concert in Manchester at the Lesser Free Trade Hall in 1976; they were instigators as well as musicians.

With the release of their debut full-length album *Another Music in a Different Kitchen* in March of 1978, their status went through the roof. They even appeared on *Top of the Pops* multiple times. It was pretty much unheard of for any alternative band from the north to achieve such national glory. It had always seemed like London had all the best groups in the early punk scene, but now, as the movement was starting to evolve, we had our very own.

Sometime around 1978, when I was about fifteen, me and Foxy went to see them in Manchester.

Up until then, I was under the impression that punk rock was a very violent affair: punching, kicking and spitting, all topped off by snarling, aggressive posturing with a venomous delivery.

This wasn't what I saw in Buzzcocks. Powerful, passionate, tuneful and melodic was my experience, delivered with such joy. Pete Shelley even smiled coyly throughout the whole set while guitarist Steve Diggle looked like he was having the time of his life. At the gig, I was sporting a black worker's jacket and Steve Diggle had the exact same one on. I was at the front and managed to catch his attention and gestured to him, showing him my attire. He looked down and gave me the thumbs-up. I was in awe.

Pete Shelley was pretty much stuck on the microphone. There was a bit of jagged and punky movement from Steve Diggle, with the bass player Steve Garvey being the most active, pogoing around the stage. But what *really* excited me was the lad at the back playing the drums, just how incredibly fucking cool he looked and sounded. I was completely gob-smacked. He had a gymnast's movement, powerful yet simultaneously filled with grace. This was John Maher. Watching the gold from his cymbals shimmer under the stage lights, coupled with his sparkling, iridescent red Premier drum kit, was one of the most beautiful things I'd ever seen.

I had fallen in love with these fuckers. That was it. I had found my calling. That's exactly what I wanted to do: play the fucking drums and be in a band like Buzzcocks.

I was told at the Virgin Records shop that there would be an album promotion for their debut album *Another Music in a Different Kitchen*. This was going to take place outside their shop on Lever Street. They would be releasing 100 balloons into the air with tickets attached. If you were lucky enough to nab one, you got a free copy of the band's new record. Not having the funds to purchase the LP, this was great news. I was gonna grab myself a free copy of that album for sure.

Me and Foxy got the bus to Piccadilly in central Manchester. Lever Street was two minutes' walk away. When we turned down Lever Street, it was absolutely mobbed.

When the balloons were released, all hell broke loose. In the frenzy to get one, somebody grabbed the string holding all the balloons. Most of them got stuck in an office overhang on Lever Street and people were climbing up the outside of the building to retrieve them. It was absolute carnage. I wasn't even close to getting a balloon. I would have to start saving.

The album, when I finally got it, became one of the greatest obsessions of my life. I pored over every inch of the sleeve, every song, every element of the artwork. They were not just the coolest band I'd ever seen, but *the coolest people* I'd ever seen in my life. Every song on the album was the best song I'd ever heard.

And on the flip side of the sleeve there was the following, typed out:

New Hormones. 182 Oxford Rd

An address in central Manchester.

I phoned Foxy. 'Come on, we're going to Oxford Road.' I had no idea what we were actually going to do when we got there, but there was always a chance of seeing or meeting my heroes. Just seeing where their management office was based was enough of a thrill.

We got off the bus at the Manchester Museum on Oxford Road. Oxford Road is one of the main thoroughfares running from the south of the city to the centre.

There was a row of Edwardian terraces – the first one was No. 188, the next No. 186. The numbers were going in the right direction ...

But the very last house on the row of terraces was 184. There were no more houses after this, just university buildings and the Phoenix, a two-storey pub/nightclub. We were completely baffled. No matter how many times we checked, the row of terraces finished at 184.

'Where the hell is 182? What utter bastards! We've been had!' I couldn't believe it.

Many years later, I told Richard Boon, the former Buzzcocks manager, my tale of woe. I said I was furious when me and Foxy got to No. 184 on Oxford Road, only to find out that there actually wasn't a No. 182.

He confirmed we'd been wrong; 182 did exist. It was in the basement of 184. *You wanker!* I thought. *You could have spelt it out a bit more clearly on the sleeve! Would calling it 184a have killed you?*

I love Richard Boon by the way.

When I later found out that the Buzzcocks management offices had moved to Newton Street in central Manchester, I decided to head out on another pilgrimage. I bunked off school and traipsed up and down that bloody road for hours and hours on end just to catch a glimpse of my heroes.

I managed to find out that Pete Shelley had a place in Gorton, a suburb about 4 miles south of Manchester and went round to his house too. I was met with a less than happy lad who answered the door. 'He's not in, fuck off!'

I fucked off.

Whenever I get approach by a Smiths fan, I remember the teenage me, practically stalking Buzzcocks around Manchester. All I can think is *I've been there, I've fucking been there! I know exactly what it means to you because I've done exactly what you've done myself.* And, of course, I tell them to piss off. Joke.

So, my love, infatuation, obsession – whatever you want to call it – for Buzzcocks, and in particular John Maher, had given me my calling in life. Fuck yeah! I wanted to be a drummer. I loved drumming! I drummed my little heart out to Buzzcocks songs in my head at school with files in metalwork class. The teacher, Mr Tranter, told me in no uncertain terms to stop being a dick and put the tools down. I ceaselessly battered out rhythms on the arm of our bright orange plastic couch in the living room with knitting needles until the plastic started to split. I guess this made me... *a drummer?*

Well, close. But still no cigar.

I wasn't intimidated about learning how to play properly or about starting a group. The punk ethic was that you did not need to be great. You just needed to be able to get on with it. To me, punk rock wasn't about the musicality. It was about the spectacle of what you were hearing, what you were saying. That's what it was about. It's been expressed many times before, but when people talk about the attitude of punk, it was just kids doing what they wanted to do rather than conforming to what was expected of musicians; the art-school technical ability, but not much in the way of heart or raw authenticity. You could express yourself without having musical dexterity or be a master of your instrument after practising and playing for ten years. I decided on the former – just get out and play and see what happens.

There was just one issue. I still didn't have any drums.

PART 2
BECOMING

9

FICK AS A BRICK

1978

One weekend, me and Mam went to Highway Music Centre. It was situated on Deansgate, right in the centre of Manchester. Every drum in the shop looked beautiful.

Ever since I had first seen John Maher play one, I had dreamt of owning a red Premier drum kit. But one look at the price and my mam took a sharp intake of breath. The two things you quickly realise about drums – the things that don't appear in your fantasies – is that 1) they're bloody inconvenient to cart around, and 2) they're bloody expensive.

The Premier range was way out of my budget, but the lad serving us said that they had a red Beverley kit for sale. I'd never heard of Beverley. But, to be fair, I'd never heard of *any* other makes besides the kit John played.

He took us over to the Beverley kit. 'Beverley' didn't sound particularly cool, not very punk. But the set was red and that was good enough for me. Besides, I was a drummer and I still needed a kit. However, after my mam caught sight of the price tag on the cymbal, she went white as a sheet before slumping into a nearby chair.

'Is it too expensive, Mam?' I asked, adopting the look of a homeless child begging for a scrap of bread to stave off my imminent starvation.

'Errrm, well, it *is* more money than I thought it was going to be...' she said.

But she couldn't bear to let me down and, later that day, the red Beverley was installed in my tiny bedroom. Who needs space for a bed when you've got a beautiful drum kit? I brought the record player upstairs and played along to anything I could get my hands on. Buzzcocks, Genesis, the Beach Boys, Leo Sayer... I didn't care whether I liked the artist or not, I was playing the drums. Truth be told, I had absolutely no idea what I was doing. I was just whacking the hell out of the kit in the most unmusical fashion. However, it felt good and that was all that mattered.

X

I suppose you would say I'm 'self-taught'. I kind of regret that I didn't start with a drumming book or take lessons. I eventually did seek out a drum tutor, but that was a few years later after I joined the Smiths. I was anxious that Johnny and Andy's musicianship was of a much higher standard than mine and decided, just after we got together in 1983, to see if formal training might be the way to help me improve my playing and hold my own in the band. I asked around to see if anyone knew of a drum tutor and I was given a lead to a guy based in Stretford. It was only a twenty-minute bus ride from my house, and he told me I only needed to bring my drumsticks. I found out later that he also gave John Maher, the drummer from Buzzcocks, lessons too. If it was good enough for John Maher, it would work for me.

After I arrived at his place, I was escorted to a small shed in his huge back garden. I noticed there were cages all around the yard. Of course, I asked him what the story was with the cages and he told me they housed exotic and wild cats. I didn't ask any further questions. We arrived at the shed where he kept his drum kit. He invited me to take the stool. He looked very much like a 'jazz head', a soggy cigarette dangling from his bottom lip and an aura of unshowered funk clinging to him in an almost visible fugue. His breath completed the particularly pungent icing on a rather grotty cake. The smell that emanated from his mouth made it clear that hygiene was not high on his list of priorities.

'Are you left or right-handed?' he asked me.

Luckily, I was right-handed, so we didn't have to move the kit. Most drummers, as most people in life, are predominantly right-handed and play the bass drum with their right foot and the hi-hat on the left. For 'lefties', it's the other way around.

'Okay, Mike. Can you just play some "time" for me, please?' he asked.

'I'm not familiar with that song, "Time",' I responded.

I looked at him with a mixture of confusion and nerves.

He released a long, loud sigh punctuating his dismay, then said, 'Just play the drums, please.'

I played for about thirty seconds and then he held his hand up. His expression was one of disappointment and slight disgust.

After a long pause, he said, 'Hmmm, your hands aren't really in the correct position and neither is your right foot. Also, you're slumped forward and not sitting correctly.'

It wasn't a great start. He showed me how to sit 'correctly' with a very straight, rigid, upright posture. He also adjusted the position of my hands. I was playing with my palms facing up and he told me to turn them so that my palms were facing downwards. It felt really awkward, but I persevered.

I practised like this at home for a while and when I went to the next Smiths rehearsal, I adopted the positioning he had recommended. Like a 'proper' drummer.

After the first song, Johnny turned to me.

'What are you *doing?!*' he demanded. 'Why are you playing like that?'

'I've been taking drum lessons,' I beamed. 'This is how the tutor told me I would become a better player.'

Johnny was brutally honest in what he thought of these 'tips'.

'It's affected your playing, but not in a good way. You're not playing with your natural style anymore that works with the songs. And … it looks shit.'

I didn't go back for a second lesson.

I don't know whether, if I had carried on down this route for six months or a year, maybe I might have seen the difference. And what difference was I looking for? Wasn't it enough that I was serving the songs in a way Johnny and the band approved of? Johnny was writing 'This Charming Man' in the morning and 'What Difference Does It Make?' in the afternoon. I didn't have time to be able to work on something over a long period; I had to try to keep up with him. Johnny once told an interviewer something along the lines of, 'If Elvis had Mike and Andy as a rhythm section, he would have been a bigger artist than he was', which is such a lovely thing to say. It's also tinged with sadness because, in the industry, a lot of fellow musicians *knew* that Andy was one of the best bass players around. But it took for him to pass for people to *really* talk about just how influential he was.

X

But anyway, back to that first drum kit.

My next-door neighbour bought a cheap guitar and we decided to start our own band with me at the ripe old age of fourteen. He was a year older. We attended a Rickie Lee Jones in concert at the Free Trade Hall in Manchester. He was just starting to learn how to play too so there wasn't a huge disparity between our level of proficiency. I didn't realise it at the time but there was a massive amount to learn in terms of timing, touch, subtlety, sympathy with the other player, etc. For now, I was playing the drums and I was in a band – albeit in my dad's shed – and that's all that mattered.

We called ourselves Amphetamine Sulphate... We discussed what we thought the chemical formula was for Amphetamine Sulphate so I could emblazon it on my bass drum head like proper bands. We thought it was, 'AsO2'. We were bloody miles out. AsO2 is arsenic.

Unsurprisingly, we were terrible. But I didn't care. Each time we were allowed to rehearse, we had to set up before getting about an hour or so to play. We then had to take all the equipment back down and 'get the hell out' of my dad's sacred space.

My neighbour was designated lead singer, if you could call it that. More shouting, really. We drafted in a local lad called John Saxon on bass. Unusually, and unlike most new bands, we didn't attempt any covers as our skills were so rudimentary, such a task would have been far out of reach. We were initially just happy jamming. However, our conviction of imminent greatness ran deep and, not before too long, we decided to take on the task of composing a song: 'Fick as a Brick'. It was as shit as it sounds.

Dad was horrified by what he saw and heard, but he bit his lip.

We thought our 'thing' was an aggressive, primal force of music and rhythm. In truth, it was just a fucking racket. I felt like we were not prac- tising enough or indeed going anywhere fast due to the constraints of available rehearsal place – and an almost complete lack of basic skill. We played together sporadically for about six months before things fell apart. But it was just enough to make me realise that this is what I wanted to do with my life.

One day, I was scanning the 'Bands, Musicians Wanted' column in the local paper, the *Manchester Evening News*, and I saw an advert: 'Punk drummer required, Manchester based. Call Ian.' Well, I was a drummer from Manchester. I was, at the very least, punk-adjacent. I fitted the bill perfectly. This will be my new band, I thought. They were called the Hoax.

I don't think I'd been playing for more than a year at this point, but my enthusiasm once again made up for any inadequacies in my ability.

I contacted Ian and went to their rehearsal space at TJ Davidson's rehearsal rooms on Little Peter Street. Although everyone in this new band were just kids, I was still the youngest by quite some way, having just turned fifteen. It didn't seem to matter to rest of the lads and it certainly didn't bother me in the slightest.

They looked so fucking cool. Ian, the singer, wouldn't have looked out of place in the Clash. He was tall and skinny, and wore bondage trousers and brothel-creepers, and was aggressive, confrontational, with a snotty attitude when performing. He was the perfect punk frontman.

The guitarist Andy was a ferocious-looking Bowie fan with a snarling pit bull of a guitar sound. Andy had the obligatory dyed-black spiked barnet and a front tooth missing. Always cool ...

Bass player Steve was a mixed-heritage lad whose style alternated between aggression and upbeat funky reggae. As soon as I heard Andy's chainsaw guitar sound, I was in heaven. Now this was what I'd been looking for. I didn't know any of the songs, but I tried my damned hardest to come up with some suitably aggressive drum parts.

And guess what? I only got the fucking gig!

After having restricted my practising at that point to my bedroom and Dad's shed, the rehearsal room at TJ Davidson's was a dream come true. Not only were there no restrictions on the volume, but there were also some pretty cool bands in the other rooms too. Buzzcocks – *BUZZCOCKS!* – occupied the best room, just by the front door. V2 were practising in there as well. They had adopted a 'glam' look, their sound an obvious nod to their love of Bowie, with a sprinkling of the New York Dolls for extra measure. I still have a copy of their cracking single, 'Man in the Box'; the cover art alone, featuring a bloke in his underpants, makes it a noteworthy release for any discerning punk collector. The bloke was actually the owner of the rehearsal rooms, Tony Davidson. They looked and sounded ace. We only got to see Tony when it was time to pay the rent. This was always a source of disagreement as Andy was the only one who ever managed to get his hands on any money.

Me, Andy Farley (guitar) and Steve Mardy (bass) of
the Hoax outside TJ Davidson's, 1979.

There was another good band that had the top space, one of the bigger rooms. They were called Joy Division and, two years later, they would record the video to their deathless single 'Love Will Tear Us Apart' in this very room, twenty days before singer Ian Curtis took his own life.

I'd only been rehearsing at TJ's with the Hoax for about a week when I was on my way to the pub around the corner to get a pie when I noticed that the door was slightly ajar to one of the rehearsal spots on the ground floor.

I stuck my nose around the corner. And there it was: the red Premier kit. Paiste cymbals angled at 180 degrees. Rack tom completely flat. John Maher's kit.

'Is this Buzzcocks' room?' I asked.

An uncharacteristically polite roadie answered in the affirmative.

There was a guitar – Shelley's Starway guitar – next to the gleaming red kit. And, next to both, a short, handwritten ten-song setlist: 'Orgasm Addict', 'What Do I Get?'... I was a boy brought up surrounded by my parents' holy relics. But here, in this old converted mill space near Deansgate station, were *my* holy relics.

The Hoax's first gig was in Ashton-under-Lyne at a pub called the Spread Eagle. I decided to put an advert in the newsagents at the end of Wilbraham Road. It was on a piece of A4 paper. I wrote in pen that the gig was a 'Rock against Racey' show, the pun a nod to the 'Rock Against Racism' show in Alexandra Park with Buzzcocks and Steel Pulse that I had recently attended. I found racism vile. But I also found Racey vile, purveyors of bubblegum pop hits such as 'Some Girls', 'Lay Your Love on Me' and also the original version of the song 'Mickey' by Toni Basil – 'Kitty'. Racey's then ubiquitous manufactured pop was the antithesis of what I felt a band should be. They were anti-punk.

The clientele at the Spread Eagle were mainly heavy rockers and their soundtrack of choice usually consisted of bands like Judas Priest and AC/DC. Their style often announced their musical taste, with their long hair and a strong affinity to denim. When I saw the crowd that night, I was alright with it, as in my experience, I found that heavy rockers and punks got on okay in the main. They never seemed to have any beef with one another. Both were outsider subcultures who appreciated a metal or leather accessory. Both were tribes always seemingly on the edge of extreme violence. One was fuelled by amphetamines, the other by real ale. A slither of tolerant respect at the centre of the Venn diagram.

The parents of our singer Ian had made the journey to the gig too. They lived in Stalybridge, just a ten-minute drive from the venue. I remembered seeing his mam with a glass of sherry in her hand, absolutely proud as punch that her son was performing a concert. Her reaction after we had started to play though is not a matter of public record.

10

A DIFFERENT KIND OF FRONTMAN

In the UK in the late '70s, it was very much frowned upon to show any sort of personal identity outside the perfunctory, straight framework. 'Individuals' stood out. Expression through fashion was considered rather shocking. 'Normal' was the order of the day. Normal wasn't threatening.

One of the first times that the Smiths were in New York, we saw a black guy rollerblading down the centre of the street with a purple Mohawk. We were like, 'Wow, look at that!' The native Manhattanites thought it was no big deal. But in Manchester, as the new decade beckoned, punks and their more glamorous progeny, the New Romantics, were a big deal. And not necessarily for the right reasons. If you were different in Manchester, you got singled out. There was an element of danger. Personal taste wasn't allowed. 'Not following the herd' was an offence punishable by vigilante beatings. Just ask Johnny Rotten.

Yet it was through punk that I was inspired to find my own identity. Spiky hair was the first thing I flirted with. I didn't have the money to buy hair products, so I had to improvise. I tried numerous free ways to get my hair to stay spiky. I used to mix sugar and water, making it into a glue-like consistency but with limited success. A punk told me to try using milk. I did and it worked pretty well, until I stayed at a girl's house one night and the next day she asked me if I'd been sick in the night. Nope, that was just the milk in my hair going sour. Undeterred, I began experimenting with other household items as styling aides. Egg whites became a favourite styling go-to, but there was a technique to it. You got an egg, cracked it open, then poured it into the other half of the shell until it separated from the yolk. You then took the egg white and threw away the yolk. The white was where it was at. You could put that in your hair and it would stay up for hours. My dad was not too pleased with this concoction when he once caught me raiding the kitchen for supplies before going out. But coagulation was preferable to curdling.

NB: Mike's Hair Tips – don't bother with soap and water when going to a gig. The sweat just activates the soap and you end up with your eyes stinging like fuck and temporary blindness. Trust me.

After I mastered the spiky hair, I ventured into punk clothing. One favourite go-to outfit was a white vest, plastic trousers and mining boots. That was enough to trigger narrow-minded town folk and also earn myself a potential beating.

Foxy and me, 1979. The egg whites were doing their job.
Note Foxy's Adam and the Ants T-shirt.

But Manchester around this time had a very controlled, segregated nightlife. The bohemians and the alternatives went to their corners and the lairy lads up for a scrap went to theirs. There was no cross-pollination between the different species. We had our clubs, they had theirs. And because the demarcation lines had been drawn, you didn't stray across the boundaries. Subsequently, everyone became a face on their own self-designated scene.

We stuck together at our own clubs and venues: Manchester Polytechnic, Rafters, Pips, the Ranch bar and post-punk Devilles and Legends. We all had an affinity with each other, often sharing the same musical and fashion interests. This wasn't your usual mainstream, high-street club crowd. You didn't need a shirt and tie to get in. They called us weirdos. We called them straights.

But all the clubs in Manchester would close at the same time, 2 o'clock in the morning. This meant thousands of people would all pile into the city centre to get the bus home. And that's when things would get a bit difficult. Directly opposite Rafters on Oxford Road was a club called – you couldn't make it up – Rotters, which catered for more of a mainstream crowd. Of course, there was going to be trouble when those punters came into contact with our lot. When the clubs closed, there'd be running battles down Market Street and Piccadilly. Central Manchester became a battleground. Gangs of 'casuals' or 'Perry boys', always liked a rumble and an excuse to use their Stanley knives.

Foxy was still my best mate at this time. Along with our shared sense of humour, we had many things in common, but most significantly we were both fans of Adam and the Ants and we had both bought the band's debut album *Dirk Wears White Sox*. It had quite an effect on me – I'd never heard music like it before. The band stood out for the way they mixed up musical styles with every song. Most punk bands were pretty fast and thrashy. Not these guys. They were thrilling and unique – rooted in punk but, at the same time, genreless. I always found it hard to place where the seemingly disparate influences came from. Vaudeville? Glam? Alternative? It was all in there.

I was particularly enthralled by the lyrical content of their songs as, unlike their contemporaries, what I wasn't hearing was 'Fuck You!' but instead something more considered and thoughtful, painting an atmosphere with words. It made me realise that punk didn't necessarily have to be who can play the fastest or shout the loudest; it could be about the ability to deliver a message in a style that was completely different from anything else around. The initial ethos of punk had been about non-conformity, not following the crowd. Now the punks had become the crowd. But what I got from the Ants and Buzzcocks was a holding of those original values. The subject matter that Adam covered in his verses was completely wild. Were Sham 69 singing about Filippo Marinetti's Futurist Manifesto? I rather think not. These words opened up a whole new world to me; I wanted to find out more.

I was, of course, also completely obsessed by Dave Barbarossa's drumming on *Dirk Wears White Sox*. He had an unusual style of playing. He was a busy player. I really liked that. Mark Laff from Generation X and John Maher have a similar style. Dave Barbarossa was another huge influence on me.

In September of 1979, Adam and the Ants were due to play at the Electric Ballroom in Camden. Another band on the bill that night that also caught my eye was Manchester's own A Certain Ratio. For the first time in my adult life, I would be going to London.

I was excited but also a bit nervous about the trip. In the late 1970s, London seemed like a different *world* from Manchester, never mind city, especially when you consider how young we were at the time. Even when I visited the capital with the Smiths some four years later, it definitely still felt like a bit of an adventure.

Armed with a couple of cans and a sandwich, Foxy and I took the direct service from Victoria bus station all the way to London. Arriving early in the evening, we took the Tube to the venue, pretending – as much to ourselves as to others – that we knew what we were doing and how to get about. Being seen as a 'tourist' would have been very uncool. We had come dressed for London – DMs, ripped T-shirts, torn jeans, spiked hair – and we didn't want anything to blow our cover. But the sights and the sounds were overwhelming and fascinating. It was the furthest south I had been.

There was already a queue snaking down Camden High Street when we arrived. London punks were milling around, smoking, posing, looking cool.

We clocked the differences in style between this southern punk brigade and our brethren back home. A lot of them were wearing kilts over their jeans in homage to one of Adam's outfits. I naturally invested in a kilt when I got back to Manchester. Some of the men had even donned make-up, which was quite startling to us. The look – one eye completely circled in black liner – was again a statement borrowed from Adam. And the hair, like on those London punk picture postcards that you still saw well past the movement's prime, came in all colours of day-glo – orange, blue, yellow and green. Of course, I'd seen people with dyed hair in Manchester, but this just seemed more extreme, more confrontational. Trying that little bit harder to shock than we did in Manchester. Heads tilted to accentuate the angles and spikes. A menagerie of posturing peacocks.

Once we were inside and Adam and the Ants hit the stage, the venue erupted. The performance was extraordinary. Adam was a contortion of theatricality. Mesmerising. Prowling. Playful. In constant motion. I'd never seen this kind of flamboyance in a lead singer before. He darted around every inch of the stage with strange, angular gestures, coupled with an array of angst-ridden countenances, constantly interacting and reacting with the fans at the front. I would see this all again in time with Morrissey. This was exactly where I belonged.

11

INTERNATIONAL STAR

I naturally thought the Hoax were the next best thing to come out of Manchester, that fame and stardom were surely just around the corner. The songs that we were writing were sounding great. We even got the opportunity to book some time in a local studio and release what would be my very first record, a single called 'Only the Blind Can See in the Dark'. Yeah? Of course it was a huge deal for me. When we got copies of the release, I held it in my arms like it was my first born. The pride I felt when I had that vinyl in my hands. I'd done it. I mean, I'd just turned sixteen and played drums on an actual record.

Emboldened by my new-found status as Manchester's premier recording artist, I accepted an invitation to Antwerp from a couple of cool-looking Belgian punk girls who I had met in the Underground record shop in the market.

It may sound crazy for a teenager to undertake such a trip by himself, but that's exactly what I did. And as for my parents? Well, they just wanted me to be happy and were not going to stand in the way of the spoilt baby and his adventures in Benelux. I got the coach from Manchester to London, then a train from Victoria to Dover, before boarding a ferry over to Ostend and then a train to Antwerp.

But if I had thought London was a bit on the edge, nothing had prepared me for what awaited in Belgium. Having rather exaggerated the international potential of the Hoax, I was quickly introduced to the girls' friends. Their crew consisted of some real hardcore punks and anarchists. The day after I arrived, they told me there was going to be a demonstration at a fascist bar in town and that I was welcome to join them.

The anti-fascists congregated, all tooled up with baseball bats, knuckle dusters and bike chains, which all seemed a bit extreme. Some members of the throng had gone so far as to show up donning full-face crash helmets. I had been expecting some booing and shouting, maybe some placards with a bit of choice language.

But what transpired next was a full-on riot. I was pretty shocked at the level of violence and just stood there shouting at the racists without really getting involved. The police arrived and everybody split up, eventually making their way back to the bar we had started at. I didn't

Oooh, you're 'ard.

have a clue what was being said, but the overwhelming feeling was one of triumph. It felt good.

I was told by the girls that they were visiting some punk friends in Geneva the next day and I was more than welcome to join them. *Bring it on*, I thought.

When we arrived in Geneva, it transpired we would be staying in old squat, four storeys high, on the outskirts of the city.

Now, this was *called* a squat, but it wasn't anything like I imagined it to be – and was certainly unlike any squat I had encountered back home. There was a cinema/film room on the top floor and a club in the basement. It was less a squat, more a happening bohemian art hang-out. After being shown my room, we left for a local bar.

There must have been maybe twenty or thirty of us in all. I was sitting at a table chatting when a few of the group we were with gathered around.

'Would you like to try this, Mike?' one of the girls asked. They showed me a piece of paper about the size of a large postage stamp.

'What is it?' I asked.

'It's a tab of acid.'

Well, I'd had a bit of speed in Manchester and tried acid, but only in microdot form. What they were offering was much bigger and, if I'm honest, looked a bit intimidating. I was not sure that this was a great idea. I was in a foreign land with people I had just met and did not speak their native tongue. The paper was put into my hand. All the other lads and girls at the table had one in their hands too.

An enthusiastic Flemish countdown began and they all necked the acid. This didn't feel good. But I was the cool punk from Manchester. Drummer in the Hoax. I had to follow suit.

All was well for about twenty minutes until I went to the toilet upstairs in the bar.

I shut the door behind me and turned around to use the loo.

But the loo was gone... I looked all around the inside of the cubicle and everything was white. A perfectly plain white cubicle with nothing else in it. I couldn't even get out as I didn't know where the door was.

I looked down at the front of my jeans and the crotch area was soaking wet. I'd pissed myself. Of course I had.

But there was worse to come ... I pulled down my jeans and realised, to my horror, that I'd only gone and shit myself too. *Oh perfect.* How the hell do I go back downstairs to the bar and deal with ... *this*? Feeling that just pulling my jeans up and fronting it out would be the most ballsy-don't-give-a-fuck-thing that I could do under the circumstances, I soon had another shock. The piss and shit had completely disappeared. It was only then that I realised this was *very* strong acid.

I went downstairs and it was complete mayhem in the bar. Everyone who had partaken was in the same state of delirium as I was.

We all gathered together and stumbled outside laughing and shrieking maniacally.

I calmly decided to just go with wherever this experience was going to take me.

We broke into a local swimming pool and everyone jumped into the water fully clothed. The police arrived and tried to get everybody out, but it was like trying to herd cats.

We couldn't be questioned by the police as not only could they not get everyone in the room in the first place, they couldn't get us to sit down, stand up, keep still or – perhaps most importantly of all – speak. All we could do was laugh. And I laughed more than I had ever done in my entire life.

When the police eventually realised there wasn't anything they could do even if they wanted to, we were all unceremoniously thrown out and we convened on a grassy hill overlooking Lake Geneva.

By this point, a semi-state of normality was returning and a peaceful calm descended on us all as we watched the sun rise over the lake. It was beautiful.

X

When I got back to Blighty, I decided that it was time for me to up sticks from the family home. I didn't fall out with Dad, but there was a tension in the air. I was getting older. I was starting to make my own way in life and have new experiences. There was more testosterone in the house.

The final straw occurred one night when he asked me to get some coal from our back garden. I snapped back at him, 'Why should I have to get it?' He looked back at me, seething with anger.

'Get the bloody coal!' he yelled. Well, I wasn't going to be spoken to like that. I – or more accurately – the *band* had recently been played by John Peel. I demanded a bit of respect. I flounced out of the house and stormed off down Wilbraham Road where I met Mam coming the other way.

'Where are you going?' she asked.

I replied, 'I'm just going to the shops, but I'm leaving home tomorrow.'

She was upset, but she knew, just like I did, that unless she wanted me and Dad rucking in the middle of the living room, it was time for me to go forth into the big wide world.

Funnily enough, the first time I went back to the house after moving out, Dad answered the door. He was over-the-top pleased to see me. When I went into the living room, he pointed to *his* big chair.

'Come on, sit down.'

'What, in *your* chair?' I asked incredulously.

'Yeah, sure. Would you be wanting a mug of tea too?' he asked. My dad had never, *ever* made me a cup of tea before. I couldn't believe how his attitude to me had changed.

I moved into a flat on Scarth Walk in Hulme, Manchester. The flat was a shithole in a shithole area. But I didn't really care though as it was *my* shithole.

12

ADULTING (KIND OF)

Hulme was a stone's throw from central Manchester and a magnet for musicians, artists and folks searching for an alternative lifestyle. It was also pretty run down. After the slum clearance was carried out in Manchester in the late 1960s, the council decided to build a vast area of high-rise crescent-shaped dwellings called 'Streets in the Sky'. It was to be the largest area of redevelopment in Europe, but ended up being a complete disaster for numerous reasons, including countless dubious health-and-safety issues.

The locality had its own unwritten yet understood rules. You could play music all night or practise the drums or entertain guests long into the night without dialling it down after 11 p.m. and people accepted it because that's what you knew you were getting into when you moved into the neighbourhood. Hulme had a high ratio of extreme characters for such a small area, all of them just doing their own thing. At one point, there was a club there called the Kitchen. I say 'club', but it was really a flat where they had knocked through the wall between the lounge and the kitchen area, making it into one large room. The DJs were set up in what used to be the actual kitchen. I never knew who owned the place or who actually lived there. I'm not sure anyone did.

The Hulme scene centred on a lot of drug-taking and a lot of music. It was pretty intense, completely illegal and unregulated – no health-and-safety checks for Hulme. Despite the nefarious undertakings, the police rarely interfered with the goings-on there. Incidents of violence necessitating police intervention were uncommon. People weren't there to cause trouble; they were there to live a more bohemian existence, however they defined what that meant. It was the 'straights' who would get drunk and fight. The police knew that if they shut something down in the area, it would just pop up again somewhere. With Hulme, everything was relatively contained.

Most of the action was set in the Hulme Crescents. These were curved blocks of flats designed to replicate the architectural style of the Royal Crescent in Bath. Each crescent was named after a celebrated English architect: Charles Barry, Robert Adam, John Nash and William Kent. Despite the glamorous and lofty inspiration, the finished buildings were poorly constructed and quickly became dilapidated. Underfloor heating was introduced but it became too costly to run, and the worst part was that it was the perfect breeding ground for mice, rats and cockroaches. It did not take long for the local government to realise their error in constructing a death-trap development. In 1974, a child fell from a gap in one of the upper balconies and died, branding the apartments unsuitable for their original purpose: housing families. After this incident, the council decided to house people in the Crescents only if they had no young children. In 1984, the council stopped charging rent to anybody that couldn't move anywhere else and, in 1993, fewer than twenty years after it was constructed, the whole place was demolished.

But despite these dangerous and less than desirable circumstances, I moved in. Ian Chambers, the singer from the Hoax, had moved into a flat and he had a spare room. The other person in the flat was called Hamrick Bryan, another Manchester lad, who held down a 9–5 job as a software engineer and never took too kindly to my musical activities in the early hours.

I made a lot of new friends during my tenure in Hulme. Skinhead Paul was an interesting character. He told me his flatmate Sean had been shooting people with an airgun from their flat window. The reason? Well, Sean was only about 5 foot 5 and had started a gang called the 5–5 Gang. Anybody over that height was deemed an enemy.

He made a mark at 5 foot 5 on a tree that ran along a path about 100 yards from their place. He'd wait at the window with the rifle for people to walk past. As they strolled by, he would check their height against the mark he'd made on the tree. Over that mark? Fair game in Sean's eyes.

We had a bad cockroach problem, though, and I don't mean those little red ones. I mean those massive, jet-black, shiny fuckers. We would enter the flat in the dark, grabbing a can of hairspray and a lighter each. Then, on the count of three, we would turn the lights on and burn the place up. The cockroaches would scatter at speed to escape our crude flame throwers.

Foxy and me at Scarth Walk, 1980. We are sitting on the very same plastic orange sofa that I battered with my drumsticks as a kid – I took it with me when I moved out.

Despite our uninvited insect roommates, I was happy. I was a man of the world, I was in a band, I had my own digs. I was seventeen and life was good.

Every night was party night in Scarth Walk because everyone that was living around there was involved in the arts or music. Everybody was doing something creative all the time.

A lot of pot was consumed in the flat, whether it be spliff, bong or pipe. Another favourite method of consumption of ours was affectionately known as 'hot knives'. The basic protocol is as follows: firstly, you remove the base from a glass bottle. This was usually done by putting a knife inside the bottle and spinning it round and round at speed before suddenly jolting the bottle downwards. The force of the knife hitting the bottom of the bottle would – miraculously – cleanly separate the base every time. Then two knives are heated up over the gas cooker flame and a small piece of dope is placed on one knife. A thumb is placed over the top of the bottle to act as a stopper, while the other red-hot knife is pressed firmly on top of the other with the dope in between both knives and put up inside the bottle. You remove your thumb and inhale the smoke that has filled the bottle. *Voila!* 'Hot Knives'!

There was no cocaine, but plenty of acid around in the form of microdots. I'd take them sometimes and go out with everybody else. Nobody would ask, 'Are you okay? Are you tripping?', as they would usually be too drunk to notice. But it would heighten any situation, making it all the more exciting and beautiful. Mainly, however, it was all about hash, Moroccan and Lebanese, and 'whizz' or speed was just so cheap that it was in regular rotation. The slang term for amphetamine, 'whizz', came from Billy Whizz, a character from the kids' comic the *Beano* who had the ability to run extraordinarily fast. I did not do much running myself, nor did I stay up for three days in a row when imbibing, but, by just taking a little bump, if you could control it and do it right, then it just made things that bit more thrilling.

So, some whizz, the occasional mushrooms, sometimes a bit of acid and lots of fuckin' pot. All the time. First thing in the morning, we would skin up; last thing at night, one for bed. You'd wake up in the night and somebody else would be downstairs that had been tripping or whatever, so you'd go and join in.

There were pubs, of course, but the only people that went there were what we called 'lifers', people that just sat in there all day, drinking. The idea of going out and meeting up with friends and having a social event at one of these establishments ... no, that's just not what those places were for. They had a roof, a toilet and a bar and that was it. They were just there for people to go and drink in. And where's the fun in that?

There was one pub called the White Horse that was different, and we adopted it as our local. It was the only decent boozer in the area. One time, Skinhead Paul said that he'd been to another pub in the Crescents called the Eagle. He said that he hung out in there on Sundays and it was great, so we decided to meet up and go inside. There were about ten old blokes in there sipping pints, ten old blokes who had lost their will to be a part of society, like they had just given up, accepted defeat and realised that there was no way back. But hey! They had a pool table! Oh, and a stripper. A stripper who it turned out also had a broken leg – a leg so thoroughly encased in plaster that she required the assistance of the landlord to help her ungraciously out of her knickers.

There was cheering from some of the blokes in the pub. I knew that she had to do this to earn a living, but the sight of it was too much. I felt a mixture of guilt and shame. The poor woman having to work the pubs as a stripper didn't sit well with me. The fact that she had to do it even before her broken leg had healed was just awful.

I went back to Hulme in about 1985 at the height of our success. Foxy was managing the White Horse and working behind the bar. But it felt different. It shouldn't have done – these were my fellow musicians and artists, the vagabonds and the avant-garde – but it did. That's what even the slightest bit of fame will do. It twists things, bends things out of all rational proportion.

By then, things had changed and it was something that I could not control. Anybody who's ever been in a band wants to be successful. That's the whole reason – you want people to buy your records, you want people to come and see you play live, you want to be able to receive money and become a rich pop star with a big house and a swimming pool and buy your mam and dad all manner of riches and stuff. That's part of the dream.

But once it gets to a certain level of success – success beyond the point you can control it – it's out of your hands. And then you only have two choices really. Jack it all in and become a recluse or carry on and watch the beast get bigger and bigger and more unwieldy. You might think you're in control of the beast, but you're not. You never are.

Come 1985 and, for Morrissey, the beast had taken control. It was pretty much impossible for him to walk the streets of Manchester unnoticed. It wasn't as bad for me. I'd get the odd bit of recognition from fans every now and then, but Morrissey was TV-famous. Caricature-famous. ITV-comedians-on-the-telly-doing-feeble-impressions-of-him-waving-the-gladioli-famous. We all wanted that level of success. We had always wanted it. But to the extent you could no longer go out? I'm not sure anybody wanted that.

13

VICTIM

1980-1981

Victim, 1981.

The Hoax only lasted a couple of years, but we'd recorded a single, been played by Peel and toured across the UK and Europe. It was a great training ground. We did the rounds of local venues that would have us, including the Cyprus Tavern. The Cyprus had a reputation – it was rough around the edges, but not especially dangerous. It certainly wasn't the Haçienda; it was a Greek-owned club that the Manchester Musicians Collective took over for their gig nights. On any given night, having ten bands on the bill wasn't unusual. And it could be a real mixed bag in terms of talent. If you didn't have a record deal or couldn't fill a bigger room, it didn't matter, you still had a stage at the Cyprus.

They served 'food', which meant they had pies sweating in a glass cabinet on a table at the back. No one ever ordered a pie and I never saw any staff member serving them up or ever touching them for that matter. But having food on the premises meant that they could get away with having a licence that allowed them to open late. A few places in Manchester did the same thing. They would have seating at the rear and have live bands or a DJ playing, which was enough to attract the punters when the pubs shut. The Cyprus was busy on Sundays because there were few other places open late. It was usually full of punks, but really anyone young and looking for a place to be when everywhere else turned the lights up would go to the Cyprus.

The somewhat weathered manageress took absolutely no shit from anyone. At the door one night, a lad asked her how much it was to get in. '50p,' she said. 'I'm not paying 50p to get in *there*,' he sneered. Quick as a flash, she coiled back her arm and smacked him across the chops with an open-handed punch, not just a cheeky slap. He reeled on his feet, staggering backwards. All of us in the queue went silent. 'Don't speak to me like that,' she spat. 'Pay your 50p or fuck off.' He paid up. That was the Cyprus in a nutshell: no nonsense, no apologies. But it was open late and it had a stage if you were in a band and had the nerve.

At one of the various gigs Hoax did in the Cyprus Tavern, I spied a girl in the crowd. When I pointed her out to Steve Mardy, the Hoax's bass player, he noted with some certainty that she was way out of my league. But I had fallen in love at first sight. I told Steve, 'You know what? That girl? I'll marry her one day'. And as I'm writing this, forty-odd years later, I'm looking across the table at *that* girl.

I moved out of Hulme and into a rented room in Whalley Range on Upper Chorlton Road with my mate Grinner in 1980. Grinner became a good mate around this time. You should choose your flatmates very carefully, and me and Grinner got on dead well. We were drinking buddies, both into punk music, went to the football, socialised a lot and now lived within walking distance of the city centre in a clean flat with a huge lounge. It was a lot less crazy than my Hulme lifestyle and I liked it that way.

I started going to Legend nightclub around 1981. After frequenting numerous dives in Manchester, Legend was absolutely mind-blowing. In most of the local haunts I frequented, if it had a bar and a roof, it was acceptable. Legend was a club like I'd never experienced before. I think the term 'super club' could describe it perfectly.

It had an incredible sound system and a lighting rig with lasers suspended above the dancefloor. Great tunes, mixing the old with the new: Soft Cell, Bauhaus, Yazoo, Bowie, Roxy, the Velvets. It was the height of New Romanticism so nobody was afraid of getting properly dressed up. A much friendlier and hedonistic vibe than the notorious Haçienda's early days. I would even see Johnny there on a few occasions.

Around 1981, I met a lad called Wes who also lived in Whalley Range and played bass in a band called Victim. I knew the band because they also used to practise at TJ's. They'd formed in Belfast in 1977 and were the first act to play the infamous Harp Bar in the city, one of the first punk venues to open in that area. The legendary Terri Hooley had signed the band to his Good Vibrations label. Rat Scabies, drummer from the

Damned, produced one of their singles, giving them instant punk cred-ibility. The whole band had come over to Manchester, only to have all their gear stolen from the back of a van. Wes and I became good mates, as I did with Joe, the singer/guitarist, and I ended up joining Victim. It was your classic punky-pop three-piece. In the summer of '81, we got a battered old Sherpa van, stuck a mattress in the back and booked a small tour across the UK with a couple of mates in tow to drive and tech. I absolutely loved touring with these lads. I even got my best mate Foxy in on the action as designated roadie. And Stan the driver was our perfect road buddy – funny as fuck and always ready to put a shift in. I loved these lads and I loved being in the band. But destiny was calling.

Me and Wes, dreaming of seeing our record on the shelves.

14

STEVEN AND JOHNNY

In the flat in Upper Chorlton Road, sporting a look that lasted
about two hours before I dyed my hair back to black.

I eventually moved out of Whalley Range and shacked up with a mate called Pete Hope. Pete was very level-headed. He was doing a post-graduate art degree and his work was strewn all over the floor of the flat. His musical taste was quite avant-garde by my standards – a lot of jazz and underground blues artists, that sort of thing. This was not my scene at all, but we got on famously. We smoked a lot of dope together and hung out on Manchester's bohemian art scene.

The flat was located on Manchester Road in Chorlton, right on the corner of Wilbraham Road, near an old pub called the Lloyds. This place was only up the road from where I was brought up. Whalley Range was a step up from the shithole flat in Hulme, but this flat in leafy suburban Chorlton was a far more sophisticated, comfortable abode. Rather than staying up all night as I would have done in the past, I could watch the locals play crown green bowls from my kitchen window on a Sunday. It was all very civilised.

Pete mentioned to me that a lad he knew called Johnny was looking for a drummer and he'd told him that I played. Johnny had given Pete a tape of some of his stuff, which we both listened to. It was completely different to anything I had played before. But it was brilliant. Unusual, certainly very cool, but brilliant. There were two songs on the cassette – 'Suffer Little Children' and 'The Hand That Rocks the Cradle'.

The tracks on the tape had been recorded at Decibel Studios a few months earlier in the year. In fact, they were put down only a matter of weeks after Johnny first met Morrissey. The origin story of the group fore-shadowed the alchemy that would eventually become apparent when the four of us finally got together. Johnny, who was then just eighteen, had been looking to form a band. Twenty-three-year-old Morrissey was a bit of a face around Manchester, known for fanzine writing and being involved in the local punk scene, most notably as the lead singer in a short-lived group called the Nosebleeds. One day in May 1982, Johnny arrived unan-nounced, but accompanied by mutual friend and fellow guitarist Stephen

Pomfret, at the Stretford house. After Morrissey answered the door, Johnny introduced himself and explained that he wanted to form a new band – with Morrissey as the singer and lyricist. Despite the unorthodox introduction, the two of them hit it off immediately. Johnny later said that he was instantly taken by Morrissey's intensity and intelligence, and Morrissey was impressed with Johnny's confidence and ambition. Johnny returned the next day, this time with his guitar in hand.

My audition took place at Spirit Studios on Tariff Street in Manchester where I was told Johnny and his bandmates were rehearsing. It was Pete who encouraged me to just go down, have a play and see what I thought.

I was going out in town with mates after the audition, so I decided to get the festivities started with a few magic mushrooms before I left the house. Nothing fucking crazy. Just a few mushrooms gently powdered, so you could just have a little half-teaspoon. Nothing too frightening or worrying or able to affect you physically or mentally; just like having a couple of big fucking shots of Jack Daniels. Just enough to get a tingle.

When I got down there, I was welcomed by Johnny and introduced to the bass player, Dale, and the singer, Steven. It was the first time I had laid eyes on Dale or Steven, but I'd seen this lad Johnny before. I recognised his face from Legend and I had definitely seen him working on the till in a local shop called X Clothes. I'd been in there a few times – the last time I was in there, I'd seen a wildly coloured jumper in orange, black and yellow angora wool, perforated with post-Westwood holes and rips. *This will look so cool*, I thought as I picked it up. Then I looked over at Johnny and his mate behind the sales counter. They were achingly cool. And in that moment, I couldn't bear the potential scorn I might encounter when we all realised – to their howling derision – that I was not entitled to wear the pullover. I put it back. I was too scared to find out what they might think.

And on this day in Spirit Studios, just like every other, Johnny looked fantastic. Intimidatingly so. He was wearing a leather coat and boots

– both authentic Johnson's branded from London's King's Road. Very expensive and way out of my league. From his perfectly coiffed barnet down, this was a lad who prided himself on looking good.

Johnny seemed like he'd been a guitarist since he was born. Aged only eighteen, he was already the veteran of four semi-serious bands. I still don't think I've ever come across anyone that suited a guitar slung over his shoulder like that kid did in 1982. Even now, Johnny doesn't play guitar, he *wears* it. Johnny was friendly and warm, but with a well-earned confidence that you couldn't ignore. When you get the chance to play with a group of musicians that you've never played with before, you want to impress, but you never want to overplay. Johnny made me feel comfortable before I'd even hit a beat. 'How's it going, mate?' he asked. We started to chat. I liked him. And I liked the fact that he seemed to like me. The cool kid from the clothes shop.

And then we started to play.

I'd never heard anyone or *anything* like Johnny before. It was unique. He sounded like four guitarists all at once. I'd never drummed to music like this before. It had a mystery to it, like it was a secret waiting to be unlocked.

The musicians that I'd worked with previously had a much more aggressive, direct, abrasive sound. Johnny was just like a fucking orchestra. With this kid, this *prodigy*, conducting the whole thing. Every instrument, every sound, every plucked string, every scraped bow, every timpani roll passed through him.

The bass player Dale Hibbert was less symphonic. Nothing about his playing really stood out to me. He was relatively new to the band, having only joined that summer. At one point during this first rehearsal, Johnny called out for him to play a twelve-bar blues riff. Dale looked at him with a lost look on his face. In an attempt to help, Johnny showed him some of the fingering on the fretboard. And while Johnny was running through this rudimentary playing, I was just sitting there thinking, *You really should be able to do that yourself, mate.* It would have been like Johnny picking up my sticks and showing me how to play a 4/4 beat.

But the guy on vocals? He was definitely a bit weird. Steven barely acknowledged my presence. He stalked up and down, back and forth, at the edge of the room, like some pasty, skinny, caged animal in a long trench coat, not saying a word. He looked up every now and again, but as soon as I tried to make eye contact or shot a glance in his direction, he would look down at the floor.

Yep, weird.

It is easy to retrofit the significance of all this in hindsight, that first rehearsal freighted with all the weight of the band's subsequent history, good and bad. But truth be told, I didn't think much more about it in the moment; it was just some awkward guy I'd just met, a singer who didn't really say much. Or fuck all to be more precise. And a bass player who couldn't really play that well but, okay, he seemed alright. At least he talked.

This wasn't the Smiths. This wasn't *Morrissey* – we all called him 'Steve' or 'Steven' back then – and this wasn't *Johnny Marr*. This was just these three lads. And as astonishing a musician as Johnny clearly was, there was no sense of this being a *moment*. But it seemed to be going all right, that was until I looked down at my bass drum pedal. The teaspoon of powdered fun was starting to kick in and very soon *Saturn V* was bending and weaving its way around my kit in manner which would have terrified the NASA scientists on the Apollo programme.

I asked Johnny if he wanted me to play anymore. He replied breezily, 'Nah, that's cool mate. Sounds great though.' *Thank fuck for that*, I thought. It could have all gone wrong if I had to play much more. I got in my rocket and left to meet my mates for the night.

The next day, Johnny phoned Pete enthusing about my playing. 'It'd be great if he'd fancy joining the band,' he told him. Pete mentioned that

I had partaken in some mushrooms before the audition and was worried about blowing it. 'Fuck,' said Johnny, 'that's some balls. We *have* to have him.' I think I only went up in his estimation at that point.

So that is when I started hanging out with Johnny. He was constantly telling me 'You've got to join our band!', but I was holding out as I was technically still in Victim. Johnny kept saying that stardom awaited his group. And even then, I think I knew he was right. There was something exceptional about Johnny's playing that was never going to be restricted to local rehearsal rooms. And the weird singer and his remarkable words? Again, they demanded a stage so much bigger and grander than his bedroom at home.

I told myself I was just moonlighting from my actual group, but I think it felt like more of an affair. It would be different if you were a guitarist playing with another band, or a saxophonist, or a cellist, or a keyboard player even, but not a drummer. You just can't have one drummer playing in two bands at the same time. Ringo never did that. Nor Charlie Watts. And certainly not John Maher. It's about 100 per cent commitment. Giving it your all. And I'm someone who has always wanted to give his everything to that *one* thing. Fifty-fifty doesn't work for me. Too half-arsed, literally. I was pretty sure that soon there would be a clash of diaries. The need to play gigs with Victim while these new guys, these *Smiths*, would need me on stage somewhere else. And I loved Victim and I loved the guys in the band. They'd been my life for a couple of years and I was scared to leave all of that behind for a new, untested entity. And anyway, I've heard a couple of great songs by this new band, but what if that's it? What if Dale is not up to it? What if the weird singer never starts talking to me? And yet...

But, of course, the thing that sealed it for me, the thing I kept coming back to was Johnny's playing. When I was in the Hoax, we wanted to sound like Buzzcocks. When I was in Victim, we wanted to sound like Buzzcocks. When I heard what Johnny was playing, Buzzcocks didn't even come into it. He was a true original. As was Morrissey. And that unique combination, that special alchemy of music and words, the poetry of the northern working class combined with a completely unique musical sound was like nothing I had ever heard. Before or since. I think the fact that I couldn't properly describe the sound to my other mates, I couldn't put them in specific box, was what helped me make up my mind. Isn't that what real magic is after all? Awe in the face of the unbelievable?

One night we were out seeing Aussie band the Church at a venue called the Gallery in Manchester, which was essentially the upstairs of a pub on Deansgate. Johnny was there with his girlfriend Angie. He was doing his usual thing, 'You gotta join the Smiths man. You're gonna be making a big mistake if you don't.'

I turned to Johnny as the band launched into their next song and said, 'Yeah, okay. I'm in.'

We bought a couple of beers to celebrate and chinked bottles. And that was it really. No thunderbolts. No freeze frame. A few drinks in a run-down pub in Manchester. That's how I officially became a Smith.

PART 3
THE SMITHS

15

FIRST GIG

1982

It was pretty apparent to me from the first rehearsal that Dale didn't quite possess that musical quality that was required if the Smiths were going to be a great band. Johnny and Morrissey clearly thought the same, but we had our first gig approaching.

We tirelessly rehearsed four songs: 'The Hand That Rocks the Cradle', 'Suffer Little Children', 'Handsome Devil' and 'I Want a Boy For My Birthday', the first three songs being Morrissey and Marr originals and 'I Want a Boy ...' being a cover of a song by all-girl US R&B group the Cookies.

4 October 1982, the Ritz, Manchester.

It was billed as 'An Evening of Pure Pleasure', which was a slightly lofty way of disguising the fact that it was essentially a music and fashion event organised by some local students. The headline act were Blue Rondo à la Turk and with their salsa, swing and cool jazz vibes, they could not have been more musically diametrically opposed to us. On top of this, the audience were also promised 'Dance and Cabaret', all for the princely sum of £3.25 in advance or £3.75 on the door. But the prestige of playing at the Ritz blinded us all to any fears of the slightly strange combination of acts on the bill. I'd never played a venue as grandiose or impressive – or as big – as this place. None of us had. Built in the 1920s Art Deco style, the beautiful dancehall had a balcony and sprung floor with a capacity of 1,500 people.

We'd brought our own mates with us, around a dozen pals to offer moral support and to cheer us on as we faced down another band's audience. Everyone was of course there to see Blue Rondo à La Turk. Or possibly cabaret turn Roxy Hart. Unlike the far better prepared zoot-suited headliners, there had been no discussion about our own stage attire. I didn't really have any 'stage wear' as such and was ready to make my Smiths debut in what I'd put on that morning. Johnny, of course, looked like a guitar hero every morning when he got out of bed so he was fine. It was the biggest gig I'd ever played. I was terrified.

We had another 'front person' with us for the gig, Morrissey's mate James Maker. This was my first encounter with one of my lead singer's friends. I had no idea why this guy was on stage with us, but it was Morrissey's idea, so I went with it. His barnet looked pretty cool and I'm pretty sure he had a suit on which helped up the glamour quota a touch. James introduced the band in French:

> *J'ai l'honneur de vous introduire the Smiths. Je crois qu'ils vont faire BOUM ici – et je suis certain que leur musique vous sera fascinant.**

And, a conceptualist from the off, Morrissey chose to lead us on stage to a recording by German art house provocateur, Klaus Nomi.

As James didn't play an instrument, he didn't really add anything to the performance. I think he was asked to be part of the proceedings to bolster Morrissey's confidence and add some kind of avant-garde

---

* Translation: 'I have the honour of introducing the Smiths. I think they're going to go BOUM here – and I'm sure their music will be fascinating to you.'

decoration. After his opening soliloquy, he danced away quite happily, shaking a pair of maracas. I have no idea whether James's appearance was welcomed by the very few of those bothering to watch. But I kind of think it looked cool.

In the end, we only played three songs – dropping the Cookies cover – but after the first one, I put my snare head through. Fucking disaster. I looked over at Blue Rondo's crew and mouthed if I could borrow their drummer's snare.

No chance.

Cheers. So much for honour among drummers. So I turned the snare over and played the underside. Not advisable unless under extreme circumstances. This was doing nothing to help my terror. I was just hoping to finish the gig with a semi-intact drum kit and not too much derision from the meagre crowd.

This would be the one and only time that bass player Dale appeared on stage with the Smiths. James Maker's presence would survive only one more show after this appearance too – although his subsequent band Raymonde would support us at future gigs and he spent his career in and out of Morrissey's orbit.

It's a shame there's no official recording of the Ritz gig, but it does allow us to perpetuate the myth: we were the dog's bollocks from day one.

It felt like a momentous early victory.

X

Johnny had met half-Irish, half-English Andy at St Augustine's Catholic Grammar School, where the two became best friends and started playing in bands together at the age of thirteen, most recently the short-lived funk band Freak Party.

Along with Johnny's Irish Catholic roots and Morrissey's immigrant family from Dublin, it seemed to me that these guys were the same as the kids I had known all my life. Despite often being unspoken, it was comforting. But it became increasingly apparent that Steven operated with a certain otherness to most people I had met. He could be shy and self-contained. I was conversely a loudmouth, talking to anyone, curious about their lives and loves. But he was just unusual. And he certainly didn't display any interest in what me or Andy were doing. When encountering new people, he did not find it necessary to engage with anyone outside of the few individuals he deemed worthy. He would not let anyone into his world, unless he specifically wanted you in it, and I did not want to pry or try to induce him to open up to me as it was obvious that wasn't what he wanted. It seemed the best way to conduct our relationship was for him to provide the boundaries. And the door was not open to us having a close relationship. He was barely talking to me through the letter box.

It was my first experience of working with such an aloof, stand-offish frontman. It seemed to go against the grain of what a frontman's role should actually be. And although it was a bit frustrating at times, I kind of admired the fact that he wouldn't just let anyone in, so to speak. I accepted his parameters, that he sought no friendship from me and, to be honest, I didn't really seek or want one from him either. My crew were worlds apart from the people that Morrissey hung around with and I was quite happy for it to stay that way. I don't recall him ever having that many mates around him and those who did pass through were of a similarly high-brow persuasion. Or that's certainly how they presented or wanted to be perceived.

In short, we just didn't have that connection in those early days. I was the drummer, he was the singer. That's it. I was comfortable with that. I wasn't going to push myself on someone who clearly wasn't interested in being a mate.

Andy had similar experiences with Morrissey. In the early days of the band, at the end of rehearsals, Andy and Morrissey would get the bus home together. Andy once told me that the conversations were just beyond stifled. They barely spoke. On one occasion, they sat next to each other in near silence. A half-empty bus and they didn't say a single word. He actually counted the lampposts that he saw out the window during the ride because it was so awkward. He said he felt like they had nothing in common. He just couldn't crack Morrissey. For all of our shared ancestral heritage, it's a miracle the band made it out of 1982 such were our apparent differences, the sense of total social dislocation from our singer and lyricist.

But as a frontperson, as a performer, Morrissey was brilliant. His lyrics and topline melodies were so good that any lack of communication in those early days could be forgiven. This was how he communicated. I think his lyrics provided him with the means – the relief and release – of being able to express the emotions he found it hard to articulate otherwise. I think Andy felt the same. Not everyone's going to be Iggy Pop, right? I expected singers to be more outgoing, more engaging on and off stage, curious about others. Morrissey was the complete opposite.

The dynamics changed gradually over the years. Maybe he just felt more comfortable in my presence. Maybe just a bit more tolerant of our differences. But also the speed at which we found such success – and all of the trials and tribulations that go with it – deepened that bond between us. Nobody else knew what it was like. A gang mentality is what keeps a steady ship. The Smiths Lads Club, if you will. But for me, that gang was nothing without one crucial member.

16

ANDY

Rourkey, the legend. London, 1983.
© Martin Joyce

An old friend of Johnny's, a lad called Tony O'Connor, was working at EMI. Tony somehow persuaded the big bosses to cough up a bit of dough, which got us some recording time at Drone Studios in Chorlton. Located just ten minutes from central Manchester, Drone was a small, 'no frills' sixteen-track set-up. Despite its simplicity, we always seemed to get pretty good results when we worked there. It was exceptionally rare for a major label such as EMI to fund demos for an unsigned act. They were interested in what we could do. They politely passed. Four years later, of course, EMI signed the Smiths just at the point of our implosion. We recorded nothing for them as a band.

Affectionately nicknamed 'The Denim Dungeon' as the walls were *plastered* in the stuff, Drone was in the basement of a house owned by a guy called Paul Roberts. Paul was notorious for his outlandish antics in and out of the studio. A 'bit of a character' in today's parlance.

I was setting up the drum kit when Johnny brought this lad I had never seen before into the room.

'Mike, this is Andy,' he announced. 'He's playing bass.'

'Oh, right. Hiya,' I exclaimed brightly. I was completely thrown by this. Despite everyone's reservations, I was still expecting Dale to be the bass player on the session.

The first thing I noticed about Andy was his shoes. He used to have these horrible things – I hated them – white Kio's, I think they were called. I wasn't exactly Mr Fashionista, but those bloody shoes. He wore them all the time. He always wore a big suede sheepskin coat too. That really suited him though. He was working in a timber yard as a way to make money, so, certainly compared to the rest of us soft-handed creatives, he was quite buff.

While the clothes may not have made the man, Andy's personality did. He had the most infectious sense of humour. Regardless of the situation, Andy couldn't stop himself being funny. From the moment he woke up until he went to bed, he was trying to entertain everyone around him. His style was typically Mancunian: he took the piss out of just about everyone and everything, taking no prisoners, regardless of whether his comments upset some people. The Mancunian way. They're not really interested in where that boundary is, or if they have sailed past it.

Andy never shied away from a chance to make people laugh, even if – especially if – the punchline or joke featured him as the fall guy. Mealtimes were his speciality with the humble napkin his prop of choice. He would often tie them around his chest, fashioning himself a DIY bra, then contort himself into silly poses to show off his 'garment' to all around. He did this in every restaurant, in every city around the world. This was often followed with the old favourite of the comedy serviette genre, the '*dead chicken*'. There was nothing that man couldn't do with a napkin.

You'd be forgiven for thinking life in the Smiths could be a bit dour. A bit austere. 'Heaven Knows I'm Miserable Now', right? But every minute spent in Andy's company was a joy. Every quirk, difference, peccadillo was pushed to Monty Python levels of absurdity until tears were rolling down both of our faces. The monotony of touring was punctured by the hilarity caused by this daft, beautiful man.

One time, on the road in mainland Europe, some fan had given us this weird porno magazine. No photos, just illustrations and cartoons. But incredibly, *anatomically*, well drawn. It was so fucking bizarre it was fascinating. We had never seen anything like it. At the end of the magazine, there's a particularly graphic picture of a guy coming. He has a speech bubble drawn out of his mouth and he is screaming, '*SPORO!*' We were like, 'What the fuck is "*Sporo*"?' Whatever, we just thought it was hilarious. We started using it in our conversations. If we saw something we liked, we would yell, 'Sporo!' Nobody knew what the fuck we were talking about, but it kept us entertained for *years*.

At the start of 2025, I was reading something about gardening. It said something about 'laying out your sporo'. I'd never heard or read anyone use this word outside of me, Andy and that weird porno mag that had coloured our language for decades. I looked it up and the literal translation is 'seed'. The gardener – and the orgasmic chap in the magazine before him – were both spreading their seed. I wished Andy was around for me to tell him.

X

When he joined us at that first session, Andy had obviously been working on the songs beforehand, but I was still gobsmacked. The two bass players I'd worked with in previous bands were pretty good musicians, but I'd never experienced playing like Andy's. It wasn't about technical ability or speed; it was more to do with his fluidity on the fretboard. He made the bass guitar *sing* the part. He really did show signs of incredible virtuosity at such an early age. He never made it look difficult or demanding. It came so easy to him; he was a natural. I've always thought that Andy would make anybody sound good. And for that, I thank you mate.

On this day, I think Andy was a bit nervous, which was probably understandable, it being his first recording session with us, just like you would at the start of any new musical venture. But if he was this good when he was nervous, how good would he sound when he had settled in?

Andy's style was immediately noticeably unique. Most bass players that I'd encountered would play the root note of the song, which in essence just adds a bass tone to the track; therefore they just occupy the low frequency on a record (there's a massive clue as to why they're called 'bass players'). But not this fella. It was almost like he was playing guitar parts, but with four strings. When we started 'Miserable Lie', I was astounded at what he was doing. The intro to the song has a slow, gentle swaying rhythm with Morrissey adding a tender vocal in an almost crooning style. When the track kicks in, it explodes in your face at double the tempo. He's pulling at the strings, he's slapping them, he's hammering them. I'd never encountered bass playing like this.

Johnny chugged and stabbed along, his screeching guitar noticeably different from the more subdued track he laid down for the finished album version. At this session, we sounded like a Mancunian version of Morrissey's beloved New York Dolls. Punky but melodic. Abrasive but oddly tender. The addition of Andy had inspired me to up my game. He was the last corner of the square.

Playing with Andy was completely natural. Dale and me, we never really had an affinity as players, which is a bit tricky when you're the rhythm section. Who knows, maybe it would have happened over time. Andy and me, however, we gelled immediately.

That said, I was still shocked and a bit embarrassed when, halfway through the session, the mournful face of Dale appeared at the control room window. It would appear I wasn't the only person who had been surprised to see Andy that day.

Johnny went to speak to him. Wait, Johnny hadn't spoken to him before the session had started to let him know his services were no longer required?

I've no idea what Johnny said to Dale that day and I didn't ask. It was a quick conversation. A swift execution and a successor seamlessly anointed. Dale out, Andy in. Unfortunately for Dale, when you've got somebody like Andy waiting in the wings, your days are numbered.

I still have the original tapes from that session. I hope someday that they can be released for the public to hear as they are pretty special.

I connected with Andy so totally on that first day; it was an inseparable bond that lasted our lifetime together, even when we were separated by geography. We shared a room together when we were on tour and, for years, Andy's face was the first thing and last thing I would see every day.

17

SO IT BEGINS

London, 1983.
© Martin Joyce

We played our second gig – and the first show with Andy – at a small bar in Manchester called Manhattan Sound on 25 January 1983. Manhattan Sound was primarily a gay club but also served as a venue for new bands, particularly on Tuesdays, when we were booked to play. The venue was tiny, with an audience of no more than thirty or forty people, but I don't remember us being that bothered. It was just good to be playing with Andy. And we sounded great. Tony Wilson was at the gig along with Richard Boon, the manager of Buzzcocks. Tony had not yet become 'Mr Manchester'; he was not yet the mover and shaker that he would become infamous as. At the time, he was just a presenter from the television who was involved in music. Factory Records had been going for the best part of five years but, an underperforming nightclub and the Joy Division records aside, it was still a relatively niche independent concern. Two months after our Manhattan Sound gig though, New Order would release 'Blue Monday'. This would change everything – for New Order, for Factory and for Manchester. Tony was close to Morrissey and close to the band and I know he loved that second gig as he told us. But Factory were going through a lot of shit at the time and I know he's always said he didn't regret not signing the Smiths for one minute. I just don't believe him!

With Richard Boon there, you would think that I may have been in awe about having the manager of my favourite band in attendance. I wasn't. His presence just reiterated my belief in our group: we deserved people of his stature to be there listening to what we were doing. It means nothing to have a crowd full of people at your gig that are some way related to you. If you go to a gig like that, it's fairly obvious when there's a lot of mums, dads, brothers and sisters in the crowd. We didn't have that at Manhattan Sound. It was just a modest but growing collection of fans.

As he had at the Ritz, James Maker joined us on the stage. After this show, James was quietly put out to pasture. I think Morrissey knew that there was only room for one frontperson.

Poster for Manhattan Sound gig.

In time, Morrissey's performance incorporated more and more theatrical twists as he grew in confidence. The specs, the flowers, the placards, the flesh. The first seeds were sown early though. Towards the end of the set, Morrissey reached into his pocket and started throwing confetti over everyone. It was only a small, low-ceilinged venue, a tiny club. The bits went everywhere. It was a simple thing to do but it had a great effect. I could see people smiling. We all became children. We didn't know he had it planned and I didn't ask him why. I didn't ask him *why* about a lot of things. And that's how it was with Morrissey. You realised early on that if he wanted you to know something, if you needed to know, he'd tell you. But if not? Forget it.

Around this time, we'd been rehearsing at Joe Moss's clothing shop Crazy Face in central Manchester. The small shop was down a set of steps on the corner of Portland Street in Chinatown, till on the left-hand side as you came in.

Joe was a bit hippy-ish in attitude. Laid back. But he used to drive one of the coolest cars I've ever seen; a Citroën DS, an absolutely killer-looking motor. There were no seatbelts, just a huge leather sofa in the front and one in the rear. You could easily fit three people in the front and four in the back.

Joe was an old-school kind of music guy and a marijuana aficionado. An instant commonality. He also knew a lot about music, from the 1940s up to present day. This was clearly something Johnny found stimulating. He liked nothing more than absorbing as much musical history as he could via Joe. He still enjoyed the education. The two of them had a strong relationship.

The idea of being in a band was difficult for a lot of Mancunians to comprehend. It wasn't considered a career option. When you said, 'I'm going to be in a band', you may as well have been saying, 'I'm going to climb Mount Everest.' You'd get the same quizzical look. It just wasn't seen as something that you'd do for a living. But when you're in a band, if you can't rehearse, you can't play.

Johnny confided to Joe that we were struggling to find somewhere regular to rehearse. That's when Joe offered us the shop. After it had closed for the day, we would push all the clothing rails to the sides and set up in the middle of the shop floor. We would have to put everything back at the end of the rehearsal just as we had found it. One drawback was that we could only practise there at the weekends and in the evenings because the place was open during working hours.

It wasn't an ideal set-up, but it was a place to practise. And it was free. It was an opportunity we couldn't miss. When you don't have a place to rehearse and you're given somewhere, it would have to be pretty awful for you to say no. Some of the spaces that I've rehearsed in have been dire. One spot in particular stands out when I was in the Hoax; we had to put planks of wood down to get through water in the flooded basement we were using at the time.

We took up practising on the top floor of the shop where the machinists made all the clothes that were subsequently sold downstairs. Although the room was full of clothing manufacturing equipment, there was enough room for us to have a cosy little set-up. We could watch each other. Learn from each other. Stare into the whites of each other's eyes. We could also leave our gear there without having to load it in and out every night which, let me tell you, as a drummer is fucking godsend.

Crazy Face felt a bit like our clubhouse and Joe was our point man and link to a cooler world. He knew people. It's how we got the gig at Manhattan Sound. He was a fascinating bloke. Calm, considered, complex. Someone who wouldn't have seemed out of place in a Kerouac novel. Someone who, when you saw him, you just knew he had a history.

He was also effortlessly stylish. He designed these Crazy Face jeans that we all wore – black with yellow stitching. They weren't skinny jeans as such, but they had a slight drainpipe cut. One of Joe's staples were light, stone-coloured Clark's desert boots, worn with the jeans and an old leather jacket on top. It was a great look.

We had a proper affinity with him. When you are that young – Johnny being eighteen and me a year older – and you have an affinity with someone in their forties like Joe was then, it's rare. People that age are dads. They're grown-ups. You want very little to do with them. But we had nothing but respect and admiration for him. We felt comfortable with him and we trusted him.

Crazy Face on Portland Street. You can see the logo in the lower left window and a rack of clothing in the window on the right.

In the beginning, Joe just sort of assumed the role of unofficial manager without any remuneration flowing back his way. There was no discussion about percentages or how long the relationship would last. And there was certainly no contract. We weren't making any money. We were just losing it. As a consequence, Joe never got paid as there was never really anything to pay him. But his generosity and paternal support were absolutely essential in how we were able to progress and develop as a band. Even when we had a rehearsal room, we couldn't hear ourselves properly because we had no PA. Joe bought us one. We had no way to get to a show. Joe gifted us a blue Renault Master van. We just wouldn't have been able to do these things without him. He injected his time and he injected his money. It was through Joe that we managed to sign to Rough Trade after he funded our early demos. He was the prime benefactor to the Smiths.

However, the dynamic between Joe and the band started to shift as he increasingly spent more and more of his cash on things like equipment and studio time. I don't think he necessarily did that to further his managerial claim, but each new generous gesture continued to blur the line between a (significant) helping hand and a vested interest. And for his sake, it would have been unfair to continue without being able to return his favours with a more structured financial payback. It's no secret that the relationship between Morrissey and Joe was strained. But do I think there was an episode where Morrissey point-blank vetoed Joe's elevation to official band manager? No, I don't think so. I think he had too much respect for Johnny – and Johnny and Joe were close. Joe was asked years later if there had been a power play to relieve him of his place as manager. Joe said he would not have got on well in the backstabbing world of the music business and he wouldn't have been the right person to take on such duties. He thought he wasn't cut out for it.

But I also think it's possible Morrissey was threatened by Joe as well as his relationship and influence over Johnny. Besides, the Smiths were this perfect unit. Introduce another element and the balance shifts. Would I go as far to say there was already a power struggle brewing between Johnny and Moz at this point? Maybe. But given the strength of characters involved, it was inevitable.

It was, however, also evident at this early stage that Morrissey wasn't necessarily always thinking in terms of the four of us but rather in terms of 'Morrissey and Marr'. He wanted him and Johnny to be the sole driving force behind the band and when anyone or anything threatened to upset that equilibrium or change that dynamic, his back went up. I think he felt that only the two of them really knew what was best for the Smiths and best for each other. And in a way, he was right. Who else came up with as many brilliant ideas for the band as the two of them did? If you do it yourself, you've only got yourself to rely on. Only your own shortcomings are exposed. And the justified confidence of Morrissey and Marr was such that 'shortcomings' was never a word they applied to themselves. Who even needs a managerial third party at all?

It would be a while of course before things fizzled out with Joe in 1983. But the die was cast. And we never got anyone in to assume that manager figure again. Morrissey especially seemed to feel as though there just wasn't anybody capable of doing the job sufficiently well. Ultimately, we were unmanageable. But as Johnny said when Joe sadly passed in 2015, 'without him there would have been no Smiths'.

X

My brother Martin came to visit me in Manchester in early 1983. He was a bit of a maverick. He had had a colourful youth. He was twelve years older than me and I still looked up to him. He'd gone to university, which was rare for working-class families back then, before moving to London to become a graphic designer.

He was the first Joyce to get the Smiths.

Joe Moss leaning on one of our early tour rentals
before he bought us the Renault.
© Peter Hope

For the first time in my life, I was doing something he was impressed by. What I was doing was credible in his eyes. It closed that age gap. The Smiths brought us together.

And as our local fame grew, he would name-drop wherever possible. 'Yeah, the Smiths? Mike Joyce – the drummer – that's my brother!' He didn't have to like us, but he did. He understood what we were all doing as

113

a band and as individuals. It meant something to him, and I was thrilled by his praise.

His admiration for the band was not shared by the rest of the family. Oh sure, they were thrilled I was starting to make something of myself, but it was all a bit alien. Even my sister Anne – who was the one who introduced me to a lot of music – thought it was a great thing but did not fully grasp what we were accomplishing. Later, when we were playing the Palace Theatre in the city, my dad came to see us play. As a traditional Irish music enthusiast, his assessment was as curt as it was cutting.

'That not music, son. It's too loud.'

I've always known that to really understand the Smiths, you've got to appreciate what Morrissey was doing lyrically. Musically, it was fundamentally a traditional set-up. Bass. Drums. Guitar. As old as rock 'n' roll itself. But lyrically, the Smiths occupied their own territory. Lazy listeners were quick to judge the seemingly morose themes. 'Girlfriend in a Coma', 'Heaven Knows I'm Miserable Now', 'Cemetry Gates'. Depressing, right?

Talk about missing the point. Yes, there was darkness, yes, it was sardonic at times, yes, there was even cruelty. But Morrissey's tongue was rammed firmly into his cheek. The language he used was like nothing else in pop music. Desolate. Handsome. Gruesome. And that's just one song! I never thought we were depressing. I always thought we were funny as fuck.

The sound of the group was unique. This wasn't ska, punk or Motown. And yet it was all of those things and more. People called it 'indie', of course, but that's really reductive. It doesn't describe the music, it only provides the context.

In the studio, the three of us were intuitive players. We'd plug in and play, free to go wherever we wanted. Reggae, punk, folk, soul – we could do it all and it would sound pretty good every time. Look at 'This Charming Man' – an early Motown track. 'Vicar in a Tutu' – a rockabilly shuffle with Bo Diddley riffs. Even with later songs like 'Last Night I Dreamt that

Mam and Dad sometime in the 1950s.

Me at the age of about five in 1969.
(CLARE BRETT)

Ackers Street in the 1970s. Our house was the second one from the end nearest to the Holy Name Church.
(COURTESY OF THE MANCHESTER SCHOOL OF ART SLIDE LIBRARY AT MANCHESTER MET SPECIAL COLLECTIONS)

Rehearsing with the Hoax in 1979. Note the red Beverley kit with the flat rack tom à la John Maher from Buzzcocks.

(right top and centre) Touring with Victim in 1981.

Me in the stairwell of Charles Barry Crescent Hulme 1981. Note the winkle-pickers that I wore the first time I met the Rileys.

Playing at the Cyprus Tavern with Victim in 1981.

Johnny, our mates Olly May, Pete Hunt and I at the services on the road in 1983.
(PETER HOPE)

Now that is what you call a quiff. This is a very early shot taken by my brother Martin, I believe at the University of London Union in 1983. Note the mic in front of Johnny, which proves just how early it is as this setup was only used for a couple of shows.
(MARTIN JOYCE)

(above and right) Early shots of the Smiths playing in London in 1983 taken by my brother Martin. He came to a lot of early shows, especially in London and all of his photos have never been publicly released. (MARTIN JOYCE)

(below) Passes and tickets from early touring in 1983, including backstage passes for our gig at Warwick University in June 1983 and our Lyceum gig in London in August 1983 and a ticket for our appearance on *Whistle Test*.

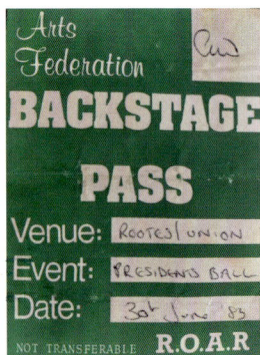

Arts Federation
BACKSTAGE PASS
Venue: ROOTES/UNION
Event: PRESIDENTS BALL
Date: 30th June '83
NOT TRANSFERABLE **R.O.A.R**

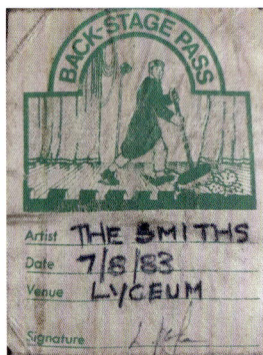

BACK-STAGE PASS
Artist THE SMITHS
Date 7/8/83
Venue LYCEUM
Signature

ASSEMBLY ROOMS, GREAT HALL
MARKET PLACE, DERBY
WHISTLE TEST ON THE ROAD
featuring 'THE SMITHS'
Evening 8.45 p.m.   Free Admission
TUESDAY
DECEMBER 6   ADMIT ONE
unreserved seating
Latecomers will not be admitted until a convenient break in the programme.
TICKETS CANNOT BE EXCHANGED OR MONEY REFUNDED
№ 987

THE ORSON FAMILY
Plus support
OCTOBER ENTS at Livvi House
FRIDAY the 14th
ADMISSION: £1.75

THE SMITHS
plus support
This most exciting new band around
FRIDAY the 21st
Admission: £2.50

The Most Exciting New Band Around', indeed! North East London Polytechnic, October 1983.

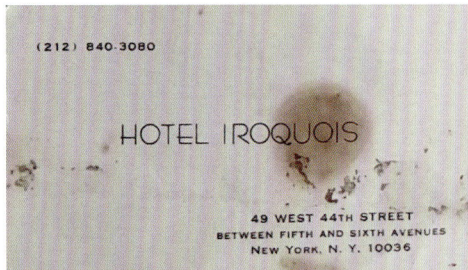

(212) 840-3080

HOTEL IROQUOIS

49 WEST 44TH STREET
BETWEEN FIFTH AND SIXTH AVENUES
NEW YORK, N. Y. 10036

Card from the Hotel Iroquois during our first trip to the US in December 1983.

More live shots taken by my brother Martin on the road in 1983. (Martin Joyce)

A quick nap before my twentieth birthday celebrations at Manchester Road, Chorlton 1983. (PETER HOPE)

Me and Foxy with Little Sean on his shoulder and Grinner and his girlfriend Jackie at the back, Manchester Road, Chorlton 1984. Both Grinner and Jackie were with me and my mate Ade when we got set upon by the gang of lads in Salford back a few years earlier. Note the poster featuring Richard Hell and the Voidoids supported by the Smiths.(PETER HOPE)

Tina and I, 1985.

On the road in Scotland in 1985.
(Nalinee Darmrong)

Andy and I in New York
before our Pier gig.

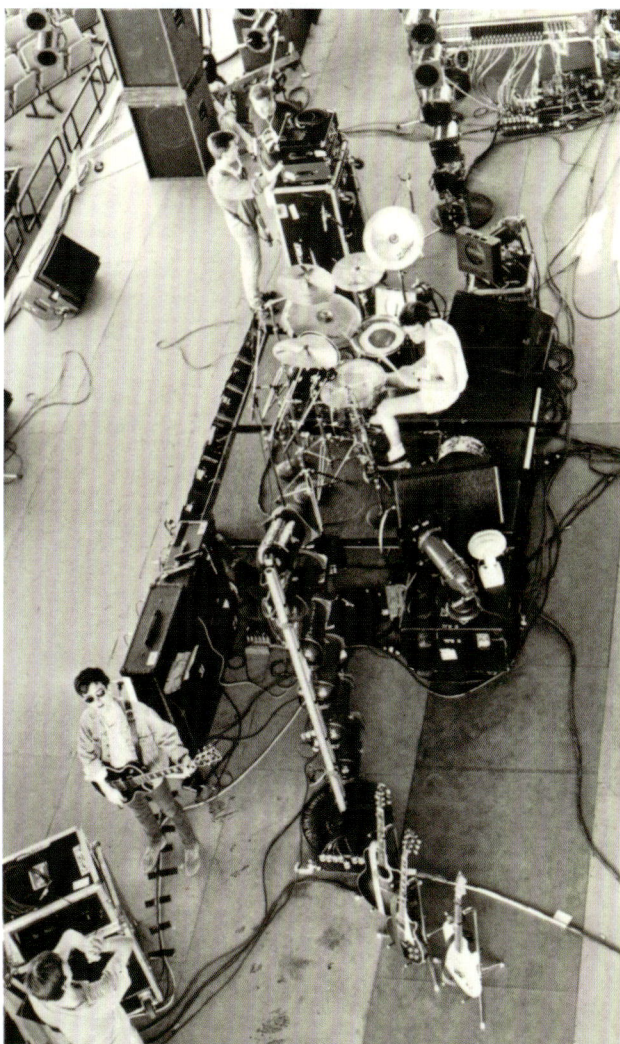
Stage setup in the US, 1986.

Beligerant ghouls
Run Manchester schools

Spineless swines, cemented minds

Sir leads the troops
jealous of youth
Same old suit since 1962
he does the military two-step
down the nape of my neck

I wanna go home
I dont want to stay
give up education
as a bad mistake

Mid-week on the playing fields
Sir thwacks you on the knees
Knees you in the groin
Elbow in the face
Bruises bigger than dinner-plates

2nd verse as 1st
except

Please excuse me from gym
I've got this cold coming on
he grabs & devours
kicks me in the showers

Image of the lyrics for 'Headmaster Ritual' that Morrissey wrote out for me, 1985.

Ticket from our Barcelona gig at Studio 54.

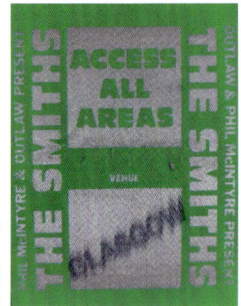

Pass from Barrowlands, July 1986. A stonker of a gig!

Image of the artwork that I have from the single that never was. 'Reel Around the Fountain' was to be our second single after 'Hand in Glove'. The artwork was confirmed and copies pressed but it was pulled.

Somebody Loved Me' or 'I Know It's Over' – the big, anthemic, string-heavy ones – they felt cinematic. Torch songs. A bit of Morricone. A bit of Scott Walker. But they never felt out of place with the rest of our repertoire because they were, fundamentally at their core, Smiths. It wasn't something we ever really worked on. It just happened. And it happened really quickly once Andy joined. As I said, intuitive. We'd mess around in the studio – maybe Andy would start playing a riff that reminded me of Big Country or the Jam, and we'd just fall into it. We could mimic the style exactly and it would sound great. John Peel once remarked that you had no idea from listening to us what our influences were. One of the greatest things about the Smiths and the one thing that is often overlooked was our versatility. We could play *anything*. And it still sounded like the Smiths. I was a huge fan.

Because of Andy's rather intricate way of playing, it was difficult for me to accent all the pushes and pulls he would incorporate without it sounding too busy or disjointed. If I did, the rhythm section would lose its flow in a song.

He pulled me up on it early. If you listen to the bassline on 'Hand in Glove', it's a perfect example of what I'm talking about. It's all over the shop. A lot of bass players play the root note of a song and the bass is more of a sonic addition to the track, adding to the 'bottom end' or bass frequency. Andy plays 'lead bass' on 'Hand in Glove' and would play like that on pretty much every track. I could never match such intricacy with my drum part; it would've sounded a mess. In the early days of us playing together, this was something that came up when we were practising. Andy pointed out to me that traditionally the bass drum pattern should marry up with the bass guitar part. We tried playing a couple of tracks in this way. A perfect example of this is 'Wonderful Woman' and, to a lesser extent, 'Reel Around the Fountain'. On these tracks, the bass drum pattern *is* following Andy's playing, but to me, it's too busy. In the end, I changed my style slightly and followed what Johnny's rhythm was doing and grooved along with that instead. That in turn left Andy the freedom to dance around the fretboard in his own inimitable way.

We used to say that you could take Andy's basslines out of any Smiths track and it would be a song in itself. Johnny clocked this and likened it to the Rolling Stones set-up with Keith and Charlie grooving together and Bill Wyman playing his thing over the top. This is quite an unusual approach for a band's rhythm section to take as it requires everyone to be incredibly tight, with each member nailing their individual part. Besides the Stones, the only time I've heard of a similar relationship between a guitarist and drummer in a band is in Siouxsie and the Banshees between Budgie the drummer and guitarist John McGeoch. If you look online at any footage of us playing, you will never, and I mean *never*, see Andy come over to me and for us to 'groove' together. Me and Johnny? We did it loads.

One of Morrissey's great strengths – and something I don't think he is given enough credit for – is his own vocal rhythm. 'Vicar in a Tutu' is a great example of this. Sometimes he follows the rhythm, at other times his vocals dance across it. 'The Headmaster Ritual' is another example, where Morrissey adopted an unusual vocal delivery to replicate the eighth notes, the quavers that I play on the snare. That rhythmic combination led to an incredibly unique sound. The sound of the Smiths.

In the very beginning when it was just the four of us, there was a purity coupled with an element of naïvety. There was nobody with studio experience involved to redirect, produce or lead the way. It helped us find our own feet. All we were doing was expressing our own talents. No producers, no record company people, no management – nobody. Just the four of us playing together. And it worked. It worked very well.

18

'HAND IN GLOVE'

What a look! London, 1983.
© Martin Joyce

By early 1983, after intense rehearsing, we had enough material to play a decent thirty-minute set:

'These Things Take Time'
'What Difference Does It Make?'
'The Hand That Rocks the Cradle'
'Handsome Devil'
'Jeane'
'What Do You See in Him?'
'Hand in Glove'
'Miserable Lie'

'Hand in Glove' had *single* written all over it. And as we hadn't had the chance to record a demo for it, we never heard what it could really sound like before we went into the studio. Until we officially laid down the single, the only time I'd heard it was when I was sitting down behind the drums and, trust me, that is not very indicative of what a record is going to sound like.

When people ask what my favourite moment in the Smiths was, I tell them the recording of our debut single is pretty much up there. We recorded the song in Strawberry Studios, in Stockport, in February of 1983. The studio is about a thirty-minute drive south from central Manchester and owned by fellow Mancs band 10cc. It was a huge deal to us. McCartney, Moody Blues and Cliff Richard had all recorded there, as had acts like Joy Division and the Ramones. It felt like a big moment. And Joe Moss, in one of his last but most significant and generous acts, fronted up the cash to pay for the studio time.

Recording at Strawberry Studios just felt like *this is it*, whereas our time at Drone was more a meeting of minds and personalities, thrashing things out to see whether or not it had that magic. By the time you're ready to record in somewhere like Strawberry Studios, you've done the groundwork. You know, at the very least, you've got that right combination.

So by the time we got to recording 'Hand in Glove' with engineer Chris Nagle, we knew we were ready, mentally and musically. It felt like a moment. *The* moment. Chris had worked with Joy Division, Buzzcocks and Magazine, so he knew what he was doing. Still, I noticed that when we started to make a bit more progress, there was some finger tapping, a bit of leg movement.

There were so many milestones with the Smiths. That recording was one of the first. 'Hand in Glove' was the first time we'd ever heard the Smiths properly – not just through a room PA, but in a real studio setting, even though we'd been together for eight months. The Drone tape didn't have overdubs. But this first official version of 'Hand in Glove' had Johnny playing harmonica at the beginning, overdubbed guitars and Morrissey's voice perfectly placed in the mix. The bassline Andy came up with for the song was just outrageous. It wouldn't have been out of place on a Stevie

The original demo from the sessions at Drone studio
in 1982 – the first time me and Andy ever met.

Wonder record, which of course is another popular misconception from those not listening close enough: we could really groove. As for the drums, I followed Johnny's rhythmical stabs at the end of each cycle.

The way we recorded 'Hand in Glove' set a template for all future studio sessions. The sound that you hear on that record is a perfect representation of the way that we played as a band. Altogether, it was a polished studio sound – and it took my breath away. I'd never heard anything like it before.

The Smiths became known for putting out tracks that were not from a specific album; that is how the compilation LPs such as *Louder Than Bombs* and *The World Won't Listen* came to be. Johnny was constantly writing and he didn't think in terms of 'this is just an album track' versus 'this is a single'. Most of the time, he didn't write with the idea of filling a quota. He just created. If a riff felt like it had the energy and shine of a single, then it became one. If it had more atmosphere or subtlety, maybe it fitted better as an album track. But we didn't sit around planning that out. He simply wrote songs and whatever came out could be either.

From my perspective, it was more about feeling: Would this track make sense as a single? Are we excited about putting it out on its own? Sometimes, sure, a song like 'This Charming Man' was obviously written to be a single – it had that bounce, that spark. But for the most part, there wasn't a strategy behind it. The music led the way.

I remember hearing about Geoff Travis at Rough Trade telling Johnny, maybe half-jokingly, 'Stop writing A-sides'. It sounds odd, but I get what he meant – he was worried that we might be burning through too many strong songs that could be saved for albums. Remember, 'How Soon is Now?' was originally released as an extra track on the single 'William, It Was Really Nothing'. Maybe he thought, *What if Johnny hits a dry spell?* But that never happened – not during the Smiths' lifetime.

19

ROUGH TRADE

Determined to get signed, Johnny and Andy went down to London, cold-calling Geoff Travis, the boss of label Rough Trade, with the tape of 'Hand in Glove' that we'd recorded. Then more successful as a distributor, Rough Trade was one of the hippest independent labels in the UK. They'd released the debut Scritti Politti album the previous year as well the likes of Aztec Camera, Cabaret Voltaire, Swell Maps, Young Marble Giants and Stiff Little Fingers. It could be a sympathetic home. But Geoff wasn't a complete stranger to the band and had already seen us play live at this stage.

I called the Crazy Face office to find out how it had gone and Liz Taylor answered the phone. Liz was a lovely girl. Ostensibly Joe's secretary, she was the first person to produce some Smiths merchandise, screen-printing our earliest T-shirts by hand – a plain white shirt with 'The Smiths' printed in black type and a bunch of yellow daffs. Liz couldn't contain herself.

'Rough Trade want to sign the band!'

Geoff Travis came up to Manchester to meet us all in the Crazy Face office and sign us. I knew we were good. So did Johnny, Andy and Morrissey. It's nice when your friends and family like you, but you hope their support is guaranteed to some degree. But when money is involved, when there is investment on the table, when there is a level of confidence from a label that they can make your records and sell them to people that you've never met, well, that feels serious. And incredible.

So, there we were, the day we were going to get a record label deal. It was our biggest achievement as a band. We had worked hard to get to this point. But it was worth it. The four of us had something special together, something that didn't quite work when you removed any one of the single elements. We were seated at a table in what passed for a meeting room next to the main office in Crazy Face, with Johnny and Morrissey sitting on one side of the table, with Geoff next to them, and Andy and myself on the other side. When it was time to actually put pen to paper, Geoff asked the fateful question. 'Well, who's going to sign? I need two signatures.' Naïvely, I took that to mean that for it to be a legally binding document, they only needed two of us. I was nineteen. No real manager, no lawyer, just a bit self-belief and enthusiasm. Johnny and Morrissey signed the document, which I considered to be on behalf of the band. I was wrong.

We never talked about who was going to be responsible for designing the album covers. With Johnny as the main songwriter and Morrissey doing lyrics, those two, by default, had the most creative input into the band. With the singer being centre stage, I think we just assumed Morrissey's role would also include the band's visual identity. He embraced it with open arms, working alongside Rough Trade's art coordinator Jo Slee to create some of the most iconic and distinctive record sleeves of the decade, of all time. They looked incredible. And just like our music, every design was unique, but every design was quintessentially Smiths. Even now, people say, 'That looks like a Smiths album'. You can identify a Smiths album at a glance. The font. The duotone colour palette. The long-forgotten cover star. There are very few bands whose albums have that same sense of instant identity.

I don't remember the first time I saw the sleeve art for the 'Hand in Glove' single. It may not have been until I was holding the finished thing in my hands. But I certainly wasn't expecting it to feature an image of a man's arse. I mean, it *is* beautiful. It's absolutely gorgeous – the silver and blue tones are stunning. It's just such a striking, classy cover. Like Michelangelo's *David*, you don't think, *Oh, he's got no strides on.* You're just drawn to the beauty of the male form.

Over the years, there has been a certain amount of historical revisionism when it comes to who and what the Smiths were. Or, more specifically, Morrissey. I did an interview not long ago with a guy from the BBC. One line of enquiry probed my opinions as to what it was like to have such an overtly gay frontman on stage. It was a daft question.

I didn't think Morrissey was overtly homosexual in anything that he did. The Smiths spoke to all outsiders, whoever you were, whatever your sexual or social persuasion. It was our great strength and great attraction. And the fact I was being asked such inane questions forty years later was tiresome and insulting and, more significantly, based on completely incorrect assumptions.

But the 'threat' some felt from Morrissey wasn't down to his perceived homosexuality but rather that articulacy that came to define him, for good or bad. It was both his greatest strength and his Achilles heel. But from the outset and during our pomp, you could never deny he knew how to give great copy. This first became apparent just after what I think was our first interview in *i-D* magazine. The February article was a promotion for 'Hand in Glove', which was released in May 1983. When the journalist came to do the interview, it wasn't with Morrissey, it was with Steven and John, Andy and Mike – just four lads from Manchester. As we were reading the story after it had been published, Johnny and Morrissey saw that the quotes we had given were attributed to the wrong people in the band. From there on in, Moz requested he do any subsequent interviews on his own, which was fine by me. And next time he would be ready. The *Sounds* interview that landed in June was the earliest example of prime Morrissey in print, holding forth with his own personal manifesto. He had opinions on everything and put-downs for anyone or anything that he felt had – or may at some point in the future – slight him. But nothing was ever off-the-cuff. He had spent his whole life preparing for this moment, writing his own personal manifesto, just waiting for the time and the medium to be able to share them with the world. Regardless of what the question would be in any interview from that point onwards, he was such an eloquent wordsmith, he would never disappoint. Peel noted that when Morrissey was on Radio 1's *Roundtable*, where he was expected to listen to and pass judgement on that week's new musical releases, it was refreshing to hear someone with such a great command of the English language. When Morrissey commented on the merits of a song, he would then sit back with a smile on his face, revelling in what he had said, looking very pleased with himself.

20

TOURING, TOURING AND MORE TOURING

Grooving away in London, 1983.
© Martin Joyce

By early spring 1983, we had played the Ritz, Manhattan Sound, the Haçienda and Rafters in our hometown in relatively short succession, so it was time to spread our wings. Our setlist was already solid with tracks like 'Back to the Old House', 'Reel Around the Fountain', 'What Difference Does It Make?', 'Handsome Devil' and 'Hand in Glove' now being performed with confidence. We were fucking tight.

We were constantly on tour, up and down the M6. Our mode of transport was our trusty Renault Master. A huge piece of board divided the interior of the van towards the back doors. That rear area was where we stored our gear. We didn't have much equipment really – Andy's bass and amp, Johnny's guitars and amps, and my drums.

Like many groups before and after us, we had tried to enhance our transit comfort by chucking an old mattress in the back. It was ridiculously dangerous because there were no seat belts or proper seating. The only other accoutrements were a boombox and an ashtray. We would all pile in. When I say all, Morrissey would always be at the front in the cab with roadie Phil Powell driving. There was seating for two passengers up front, but it was a squeeze. It was more fun in the back anyway. Phil was an old school mate of Johnny and Andy and became a very good friend of mine too. He went on to work with Johnny post-Smiths and I still keep in touch with him. He was there for it all.

A window looked out from the cab into our mobile makeshift 'lounge'. The three of us would be listening to cassettes, usually with Johnny playing DJ. We would be on the cigarettes and pot, stuffing our stoned faces with all kinds of shit food – chocolate, crisps, sarnies. If the service station had it, we ate it.

Morrissey, on the other hand, was in his cab sanctuary up front. He was (justifiably so) always worried about inhaling second-hand smoke and had the window open all the time as the three of us smoked like chimneys. I was fascinated by how he would eat an apple. It would take him about twenty minutes. In contrast, everything in the back would get devoured immediately due to the munchies brought on by smoking copious amounts of weed – all while Morrissey was just there nibbling on an apple.

If our rapid ascension in our hometown was in danger of going to our heads, the opportunity to venture south down the M6 soon brought us back down to earth. There was no 'Hello London!' in front of thousands of adoring fans for us just yet. The release of 'Hand in Glove' was still a few months off and the reality of touring life for the time being meant playing in subterranean bunkers on make-shift stages.

Our first show in London was at the Rock Garden in March. The venue was legendary, having hosted shows by U2, Talking Heads and Adam and the Ants. It felt like a transformational moment to get booked to play there down in the capital. But when we arrived, the venue was not *quite* what we had expected it would be. The 'Garden' was actually a small, sweaty room located in the basement of a building off Covent Garden. The audience was mostly made up of tourists wearing backpacks who had probably stumbled across the place and obviously never heard of us. We suddenly had the realisation that, outside of our home turf, we still had a long way to go in terms of building our name. It was not quite the triumphant spectacle announcing our arrival in the capital that we had hoped it would be.

We had a similar experience later in the year at another infamous venue on the circuit, Bath's Moles Club. As we pulled up outside the address we had been given for the show, I looked around, thinking, *Where's the venue?* All we could see was a small, unassuming building on a bog-standard street in the centre of Bath. There was nowhere to park the van, so we had to leave it down the road. With some trepidation, we opened the door, walked down some stairs and into a tiny, dark subterranean room. The ceilings were low, the claustrophobic feeling intensified by the bare brick walls. We heard the little ding of a bell on the door, alerting the staff to our presence. Once our eyes adjusted to the light, we realised we were standing in a kind of café. We looked around the room then at each other.

Morrissey at Moles Club.
© Martin Joyce

When we asked where we would be playing, the bartender proudly expanded his arm and proclaimed, 'This is it! Don't worry – we'll just push the chairs and tables to one side.'

'Where's the stage?' I asked.

The lad pointed to an open space at the back of the room. This wasn't a stage. It was just an empty bit of floor where the tables weren't.

X

Despite our prodigious appetite for weed, the thing about the Smiths was that all this extracurricular group activity was undertaken in a very controlled way. And with Morrissey a relatively abstentious presence in our ranks, I think we were more careful about how we behaved. If the lead singer is off his face every night, it kind of sets the tone. But this was never the case for us.

For us, we mainly just smoked a lot of pot. As a lot of pot smokers know, you don't really drink much when you're smoking. We'd get stoned, but because we were working, there weren't any big sessions. In the main, we drank in moderation. When we did have a bit of a blowout, it was only if there wasn't a studio session, show or promotional duties the next day. It was quite sensible, even if we weren't exactly grown-ups; Morrissey was the oldest of our lot, being all of twenty-four years old, with Andy and Johnny still just nineteen and me having now got two decades under my belt. Though we were young, we knew if we were too hungover or couldn't play, it would show. People would notice.

The same applied to going on stage. I have never gone on stage under the influence. Not once. Never drunk, never stoned. I can't do it. Besides, that rush you get on stage is the most incredible feeling in the world. Nothing can top that.

One notable exception came from Morrissey himself when we played the Electric Ballroom in late 1983. We had played on the Camden venue's iconic stage in May earlier that year, supporting none other than the Fall, but this time round, Morrissey decided to knock back a few glasses of red wine before taking to the stage – not a huge amount, but definitely more than he usually would. By the time we went out, he was tipsy. Not drunk, not falling over or anything, just a little bit more than tipsy. A couple of tracks in, we launched into 'Barbarism Begins at Home', which was the first time that we had played it together live. In rehearsals, we'd never played it in its full length.

We'd always wait for Morrissey to cue the end for that song. He'd be

Ticket from our Electric Ballroom gig supporting the Fall.

yodelling, improvising vocals, doing all the vocal flourishes and we'd just groove along behind him. Usually, his cue to wrap up would be this upward vocal inflection – a yelp – he'd go *up*, and then we'd play through another eight bars or so and finish. But that night, he didn't stop. He just kept going. We were all waiting for the cue and it never came. I was absolutely knackered and it took everything out of me. It ended up the length of a couple of our usual songs back then.

There is a surprisingly good bootleg recording of that gig available that I found online recently and you can very clearly hear the effects of the red wine with Morrissey engaging in way more chit-chat with the crowd between the tracks than he would usually have attempted.

21

JOHN PEEL

O nce we were signed, the promotions guy at Rough Trade, Scott Piering, started rustling up tastemakers across the industry to come to see our shows. Scott was a lovely guy who had moved over from America in 1980 and set up and subsequently ran the press department at Rough Trade. I really dug Scott. He became part of a small, trusted group of figures at Rough Trade who, while not officially appointed, acted with sound managerial intent. He was about ten or fifteen years older than us, probably only in his thirties, but when you're nineteen or twenty, anybody over twenty-five is ancient. I used to think that Morrissey was an old man at twenty-three. But being an American also gave Scott a certain transatlantic authority. I assumed he just must know everything. After helping us, he went on to work with some of the biggest acts in the UK – the KLF, Pulp, Underworld and Stereophonics to name a few. His was the voice that intoned 'Ladies and gentlemen, the KLF have now left the music business' after their incendiary, machine gun-toting 1992 BRIT Awards appearance.

Scott had a certain catchphrase that he used all the time, an old plugger's trick that bought him more time while examining the room. Ask him any question and the answer was always the same: 'Maybe ... maybe not'. As the old phrase goes, 'fools rush in'. Scott was no fool.

When Scott passed away in 2000, we went to his service. It was a humanitarian affair but it still took place in a church. It was a really warm, touching send-off. A load of people attended and said some beautiful things about him. Right at the very end, as the curtain was about to close around his coffin, the KLF single 'Last Train to Trancentral' began playing. Scott's voice filled the church, opening the record as it did, proclaiming, 'Okay, everybody lie down on the floor and keep calm'. The stadium house banger blasted off the walls as his coffin gently slid away. Having had a bit of time to make some arrangements before he died, he played his final hand as a plugger for the most important concluding bit of promotion of his life: his own death. He always knew how to make an impression.

X

Scott was well-connected with all the major power brokers in the music business, anyone who could make or break a band's career. Two weeks after the Electric Ballroom gig, we played at the University of London Union. Scott invited John Walters – the producer for John Peel – to the show. Walters loved the gig and offered us a session on Peel's show. Peel was always quick to credit Walters with actually discovering the Smiths and bringing us to his attention. But Peel was The Man. His approval meant everything to a young band and his endorsement could change their whole trajectory. His show was the home of the esoteric. He was the champion of the independent and to be offered a Peel session was like being given papal approval. It created instant credibility. It also meant we'd be recording at the BBC. Even my dad could appreciate that. Growing up, channels like ITV were for the working class. *Coronation Street, World of Sport, George and Mildred.* The BBC was for posh people. We were storming the barricades. It was a dream come true. Ultimately, we did a number of recordings for him, eventually releasing *Hatful of Hollow*, featuring some of the sessions we did for the BBC that weren't released elsewhere.

There's a lot of pressure when you do anything with the BBC. The process of recording a track that can take days to perfect has to be completed in one day. For a session, three tracks need to be recorded, mixed and ready for broadcasting in that tight time frame.

The BBC then was still a very old-school institution. The Peel sessions were all recorded at Maida Vale, the BBC's beautiful old Art Deco studio in west London. Having been the centre of the BBC's news operations during the Second World War, it had to be rebuilt after taking a direct hit. The BBC Symphony Orchestra continued to use it as its home after the war and, in the late 1950s, the BBC Radiophonic Workshop was set up and remained there for forty years. The place was steeped in history. And we would be part of that.

One of the things that always stood out about a visit to the Beeb was going to the in-house canteen. After we'd set up the equipment and got a sound together for any of our BBC sessions, we'd have a break for lunch before we started recording. You could have a slap-up meal for about 30p. That's where the licence fee was going.

We did seven sessions in total at the BBC down the years, including four for Peel, but around the time of our second BBC session for him in September 1983, there had been a lot of recent press interest in the lyrical content of some of our releases. Morrissey's reputation as a poetic and also slightly provocative lyricist was getting a lot of attention. Certain assumptions were made and the BBC were on high alert to make sure the lyrics didn't transgress their strict on-air policies.

Partway through the session, Morrissey walked in to do the vocal over the track that had been recorded for 'This Night Has Opened My Eyes'. After the first line was sung, 'In a river the colour of lead, immerse the baby's head...', the producer immediately cut in. 'Stop, stop there, stop. Hold on a minute, hold on a minute, stop the tape,' he exclaimed. He sternly told Morrissey that he needed to write down the lyrics. 'We're just going to review these and make sure everything is okay for us to proceed.'

The red flag had been raised. The session was halted to see if the lyrical content would cause offence among the masses and lead to a deluge of complaints from concerned licence fee payers. The lyrics were finally approved and we were free to proceed.

22

CANNOCK CHASE

We played a gig at Cannock Park in Cannock Chase, Staffordshire, the day after my birthday on 2 June 1983. I'd never heard of the place, even though it was only an hour's drive from Manchester. All that we had been told was that we would be appearing at what was described to us as some kind of festival. We shouldn't have even been there. It was one of those shows where we were asked to play and we said, 'Yeah, okay.' When you hear 'festival', you think Glastonbury. But I know *now* there is a difference between Glastonbury and a 'festival' in the park around the corner, which just turns out to be a stage and a hot dog stand on a playing field. But back then, if you were promising a 'festival', I was essentially expecting Woodstock.

We arrived in the afternoon and found that there was no catering. To add to the indignity, we would be sharing the bill with a couple of bands called Shambolic Climate and A Dog Named Ego. After scoping out the locality, it was decided that a voyage to a nearby pub would be the best option for obtaining some food. It soon became apparent we did not look like the locals. We were, as they say, not from round these parts. I never thought that we looked *that* weird or strange in our choice of clothing. We basically wore jeans, T-shirts and jackets. The odd cardigan here and there. I think the one stand-out sartorial choice around this time would be Morrissey's shirts. He'd taken to purchasing these from Evans Outsize in Manchester, a shop that sold plus-size clothing. I think it was our hair

Official poster for the 'Cannock Gala'. We are listed as
the top act in the 'rock concert' in the bottom right.

– quiffed, pomped and preened – that made the locals jittery. That and
our rock-star shades.

We were a gang, sartorially speaking, and we all kind of looked the
same. Morrissey's hair especially was a showstopper, standing several
inches above his head. The amount of hairspray we used was insane. If
the quiff wasn't sharp, we'd just spray it up. When we would arrive at a
place, even in Manchester, we'd draw glances because we looked a bit
rockabilly. But in a traditional suburban town like Cannock, which was
like something out of *The Land That Time Forgot*, we were basically aliens.
These guys were still coming to terms with the threat of Beatlemania.
They liked their subversion a bit more traditional. Real ale. Long hair.
Beards. Our look – and our arrival en masse – was not acceptable.

As we traipsed into the boozer, we were met with a mixture of horror
and confusion by those deep into their pints. It was almost cinematic. The
pool balls on the table stopped rolling. The music on the jukebox cut out.

There was just silence as we walked into the bar, everyone looking at us, clearly thinking, *What the hell is this?*

Once you have a distinctive or unique look, some people see it as a threat. They don't like things to be *different*. Right away, you're seen as a freak, a weirdo – and those tags in some places can be dangerous.

By simply walking into this place, we had upset the equilibrium. People were just having a bit of lunch, or a beer, keeping to themselves. It was clear that we weren't welcome.

'Are you serving food?' I asked.

We could clearly see that they were, as the other patrons were noshing on various combinations of the traditional Ploughman's ingredients they had on display in a glass cabinet by the bar.

The guy at the counter looked over his shoulder, scanned the group comprising the band, crew and our entourage of friends – making a total of about ten of us – and answered very firmly:

'No.'

He then added for good measure, 'We're not serving any drinks, either.'

Just like armies, bands – and especially their road crew – march on their stomachs. It was going to be a long day.

However, things were soon to get even worse once the actual festival was declared open. The proceedings commenced with a welcome from Colin Welland, British film royalty, best known for writing the 1981 Oscar-winning classic *Chariots of Fire*. He received a rousing if already slightly weary response from the crowd. This didn't feel good. It turned out the event was actually some sort of miners' gala, a show of solidarity for the mining unions working to keep the pits alive in the face of Thatcher's vandalism. In other parts of the park, trade union officials and labour counsellors were firing up the passions of young working-class men – a principle and position I wholeheartedly subscribed to, especially as my dad had spent most of his working life down the pits. Elsewhere in the park, there was a funfair, a 'Grand Gala Draw', some magicians and a baby show. But we were there as part of the main entertainment. So get on stage and entertain, boys! The term 'stage' was a bit grand, of course, as it basically comprised a number of planks laid out on the grass in a makeshift tent, but who were we going to take it up with? The threatening congregation of long-haired, bearded fellas who'd taken up their position mere feet in front of us? No thanks, the facilities were *fine*.

The atmosphere was tense before we had even played a note. Often in that situation the adversity can spur you on, that 'Right, we'll show you!' attitude before you attempt to win people round. But there's a fine line between adversity and hostility, and the initial reaction which started as mild bewilderment quickly escalated to hatred and anger. It was hard to concentrate.

The barrage of abuse primarily directed at Morrissey grew as the set progressed and by the time we got to our sixth number – the live debut of 'Wonderful Woman' – the first flying pint pot hit the stage. And that's when things turned *really* nasty. Bottles and glass started raining down. From the back of the tent, I saw uniformed police entering the fray. Incredibly, we'd managed seven songs, but as I counted us in for 'Miserable Lie', the police made their way onto the stage. We were escorted out for our own safety. I jumped into my flatmate Pete Hope's Mini Cooper and we got the fuck out of there as quickly as we could.

But the show must go on as we're often reminded and we had another gig the next night at a pub in Moseley, Birmingham. It was called the Fighting Cocks.

God help us.

Ever since, every time I'm driving back from London and get to just north of Birmingham, and I see the turn off for 'Cannock', a shiver runs down my spine.

23

THE BIRTH OF MORRISSEY

Morrissey, London, 1983.
© Martin Joyce

We'd never heard of the Fighting Cocks of course, but we were excited to play in Birmingham for the first time. On the drive over, we were all sitting in the van. At this time, we all still called our lead singer 'Steve', even if, professionally at least, his surname was already being more prominently used. During a lull in conversation, Steve told us, 'I don't want any of you to call me Steven anymore.' He paused and looked at each of us, then continued: 'From now on, I just want to be called Morrissey.'

If it had been me asking for a sudden change in what my mates called me, I might have been a bit more forthcoming in my reasoning. You know, something like: 'I have always hated the name Michael and I would much rather just be called Joyce. Let's just try that, lads. Can we just call me Joyce for a bit and see how comfortable you are with it?' But Morrissey didn't give any explanation I don't think he ever felt he had to give an explanation about anything if he didn't want to; he just announced it in a 'Henceforth, you shall call me *Morrissey*' manner. It was probably always part of that manifesto of his. But ultimately we just carried on smoking and listening to music.

X

We always seemed to be in the capital doing something that summer – we played six London shows across three months alone – but in July 1983 we were back to specifically record our debut album at Elephant Studios in Wapping. Geoff Travis had secured Troy Tate, a fellow northerner and formerly of the Teardrop Explodes, in the producer role.

We all liked Elephant Studios; there was a good feel to the place. But it was absolutely boiling hot during those weeks, even in the evenings. It was the hottest July on record. We worked quite sociable hours, ten in the morning until the early evening. But when we would return to the van, it had been sitting baking in the boiling sun outside the studio for the entire day. Our 'lounge' would be sweltering and unbearable, so on the drive back to our hotel, we would keep the large side door open trying to get some cooler air circulating. Needless to say, we did not have much time for health and safety compliance.

We'd spend a day recording, then head back to the Imperial Hotel for a beer and then head to bed. Wake up. Repeat. We never went out as a group, never explored the capital together or mixed with other musicians. We were quite insular in that respect. But we were also quite focused. We were there to do a job.

We recorded fourteen tracks with Troy with the intention that ten of them would make the album – which at that point had the tentative title of *The Hand That Rocks the Cradle* – leaving the remainder for A and B sides. The songs were never mixed. Johnny and Morrissey made the executive decision together to end the relationship with Troy, but it always felt to me like this was being driven more by Morrissey. Johnny even suggested that the heat was making it hard to keep our instruments in tune. Geoff Travis freaked out when he heard that we wanted to shelve the initial effort and start again. But regardless of the costs that had to be written off, Geoff suggested producer John Porter could try to salvage the sessions by remixing or re-recording some of the tracks. At a cost of another £6,000, John decided that the only option was to re-record the whole thing.

Personally, I really liked the versions we put down with Troy. Some of those takes were a bit more aggressive, a bit closer to our live sound and I thought it was important to capture that energy. I listened to an old cassette with these sessions recently. They were really pretty good for an album we ended up scrapping.

In August, we were back in London for two headline shows, the second of which was at the legendary Dingwalls overlooking Camden Lock. We loved Camden with its vibrant market with vintage clothing, second-hand records and bric-a-brac stalls. And the people were *our* people. Musicians, bohemians, artists. Mozzer loved it so much he ended up moving to the outskirts of Camden and neighbouring Primrose Hill when the band split in 1987.

It was a good turnout. And it was an absolute sweat box. So hot that I struggled to finish one of our fastest songs, 'Miserable Lie'. The crowd were sucking all of the oxygen out of the room.

And one thing happened that night that I had never experienced before – and have never experienced since. We were playing the slower 'I Don't Owe You Anything' mid set. It sounded *wonderful*. Johnny's upstrokes married perfectly with my snare. Andy's hands danced across his bass, the fluidity of his playing causing the song to sway back and forth. And Morrissey delivered just one of his best-ever performances; the heartfelt angst delivered in his words was perfect. You could feel the crowd utterly absorbed in the moment too. And before I knew it, I was consumed with wave upon wave of this overwhelming sense of emotion. And then it happened. My lips started trembling. Slowly at first but building until I could no longer contain the emotion. Tears started streaming down my face. It was a strange sensation, a combination of deep sadness and unbridled joy.

When the song ended, I tried really hard to keep it together. There was a split-second pause before the crowd started to applaud. But the applause was different – more muted and heartfelt. It seemed to suggest we'd *all* been transported somewhere. In that moment, we were all Smiths fans together.

'Oh, but I know what will make you smile tonight.'

I buried my head in my towel and tried to compose myself. I don't think the rest of the band noticed the utterly overwhelming experience I'd just played through and we got straight into the next song. And did I mention it afterwards? What, to three sarky piss takers from Manchester? Don't be stupid.

But from this point on, when fans would tell me how deeply moved they were by our music, I knew *exactly* what they meant.

God, I loved that band.

24

THE SMITHS

September 1983. We started to record our debut album for the second time. Rather than London, this time round we would be recording a little closer to home at Pluto Studios in Manchester. One thing you learn quite quickly about producers is that, more often than not, the role is about mediation and manipulation. A good producer is not there to teach you *how* to play your instrument better, but they will encourage and nurture you in a way that helps you to play differently. The producer is there to coax the best performance possible out of the players. But with the Smiths, up until that point, I felt that all we needed was someone to record the songs how they sounded. As far as I was concerned, they were already perfect. And then we started working with John Porter.

We first met John when we went in to record our second session for David 'Kid' Jensen at Radio 1. Jensen, a Canadian ex-pat, was a contemporary and friend of John Peel's. They shared a similar humour and a love of the same popular music. The version of 'Accept Yourself' that was recorded for this Jensen session was the one that ended up on *Hatful of Hollow* the following year. However, our take of 'Reel Around the Fountain' recorded the same day did not as successfully outmanoeuvre the BBC censors as 'This Night Has Opened My Eyes' had previously done. It was banned for two years. But John Porter was a lovely guy. Having played bass on *For Your Pleasure*, the seminal second album by Roxy Music – and then *declined* a permanent role in the band – I was both in awe and

143

slightly intimidated. I mean, how good must you be to be able to turn down Roxy?!

It was Geoff's idea to bring in John and as soon as he arrived in the studio, the dynamic changed instantly: it wasn't just the four of us anymore; we were now five. Songs that came to be seen as being among our defining works – 'This Charming Man' and, perhaps more notably, 'How Soon is Now?' – were skilfully and sympathetically delivered into the world by John.

Sessions started in Pluto before the final touches were added at Eden Studios in Chiswick, west London. John had an immediate bond with Johnny, socially as well as musically. There's never been any doubt in my mind that Johnny was a genius, but John worked really closely with him to tease out the best sounds, the best takes. They'd stay in the studio all night getting stoned and laying down guitar track after guitar track. As a consequence, I think Morrissey felt a bit sidelined.

I'm of the opinion that most singers need to be made to feel they are always the most important person in the room. And our band was no different. And even though John always wanted the best out of Morrissey, he could never be as hands-on as he was with Johnny. If your singer delivers perfect take after perfect take, what's the producer to do? You just applaud it and move on. That's the dream, right? But the voice wasn't John's instrument. The guitar was. And inevitably the disproportionate amount of time he and Johnny spent together, teasing ever more incredible ideas together out of their instruments was bound to have an impact on Morrissey.

Personality-wise, I just think they didn't gel. There was never really any open communication between the two. So even parking the practicalities of working with Johnny – tone, effects, reverb, that sort of thing – I think he also just simply preferred hanging out with him.

People talk about 'musical differences' being the cause of splits, but 99 per cent of the time that's not the case at all. It's personal differences.

People grow up, they grow apart, they fall out, their perspectives change. They just can't be in the same room any longer. And just think about how heated and intense it can be in the studio. But that never looks as good in a statement. We were still a good few years off our own personal, complicated tensions, which would ultimately irrevocably tear us apart. For now, conversely, our differing personalities would just 'make for interesting chemistry'. As Johnny later said, any tension arose from our desire for perfection as we imagined it.

Me and John had a difference of opinion over the drums on 'What Difference Does It Make?'. On the original Troy Tate version, the drums were really busy. A kind of a shuffling thing, really full, fat and rhythmical. But when we were putting the drums down in the studio, John said to me, 'I think you should simplify the drumbeat.' He just told me to play it straight. If I played it straight – *kick*–*snare*–*kick*–*snare* – we would have a hit he said. Now, if Johnny or Morrissey had been unhappy with the original drum part at any point, we would have discussed it and, if they wanted it straight, I would have given it to them straight. No questions. But when we started recording *The Smiths*, John was trying to create his own specific sound and I just wasn't ready for that yet.

It was the first time I'd really been *conducted* by an outside source and I wasn't very comfortable with it. I wanted to play the way I played. Being told to play something that wasn't in my natural style didn't make me feel great. It was a non-Smiths' interpretation of how the drums should be. And, believe me, since I'd joined the band, I had already had to learn a completely new way of playing and learn quickly. When I started with the band, I had three speeds: fast, faster and fastest. That was pretty much it. Being a punk drummer, that's all I really needed to know. There was no 'Reel Around the Fountain', no 'Suffer Little Children', no 'I Don't Owe You Anything' when I was playing with the Hoax or Victim. Sometimes I found it a little difficult to navigate. And on top of that, just imagine the speed at which Johnny and Morrissey were turning out classic after classic. They kept raising the bar and I kept having to meet it.

And the drummers that John had played with were out of this world. The drummer from Roxy Music, Paul Thompson – my God, he was one of the best drummers I'd heard. I knew what I was up against and I felt like I couldn't really come up with what he wanted from me. I think he probably found that quite frustrating. And I found it eroding my confidence.

There were a couple of particularly difficult sessions a few years later; recording 'Shakespeare's Sister' was one of them. I was in the studio, trying to nail the same part repeatedly. John would just keep telling me 'Try it again, try it again'. No more instruction than that. I eventually went up to the control room and John was sitting there, exasperated, with his head in his hands. I just found it such a hard part to play. And I guess John was just thinking, *Well, what do we do* now? *Mike's the drummer.*

In the past, producers would just bring some session guys in if you were having problems. Don't forget, even George Martin brought in a session player to replace Ringo on the first Beatles single because he didn't think he was up to it!

Luckily this never happened with the Smiths. I persevered. And when I *did* get it right, John Porter hugged me and said, 'Thank God! *Thank* you and well done.' It was hard, but we got there in the end. And while this didn't happen with every song, I was always aware of the pressure.

People often talk about our rhythm section being great, but I felt as though Andy's ability was streets ahead of mine. I felt quite intimidated by his playing, especially when Johnny would come along with a new tune and Andy would just lock into it immediately with an incredible bassline. Not, 'Oh, let me try it like *this*' or 'Maybe I should try it like that' or 'How about if I do that bit like this?' He'd just start playing the bassline immediately. He was one of the greats.

By playing things that were a little bit *different*, rather than something technically on point, I was able to keep up. Because of my naïvety, I had the freedom to experiment and do things that I felt were right for each song, instead of being beholden to some sort of rule book. I wasn't that much of a technician. I never have been. I'm still not considered a technician as a player. But I've always been able to play what I think is *right* for the song and I think I've always served them well.

Just after the album's release, I heard 'What Difference Does It Make?' being played on the waltzers when I was at the local funfair. It sounded fantastic. John's input into *The Smiths* was, overall, pretty incredible. He was right, too. 'What Difference Does It Make?' *did* become a hit, going to number twelve on the UK charts. But personally, I always preferred the original. And I know Morrissey agrees. I remember somebody telling me about Morrissey talking about that song in an interview and saying that he thought that John Porter ruined it, noting how in the original version, 'The drums were powerful … They were magnificent. They were forceful.'*

---

* Fortunately, both versions exist across *The Smiths* and *Hatful of Hollow*, and I know which one *I* prefer.

25

THE HAÇ AND
TOP OF THE POPS

Tour advert from 1983. See Haçienda listing at bottom.

We played the Haçienda three times in total in 1983. Originally a yacht showroom on Whitworth Street, the Haç was a cavernous building, designed by Ben Kelly and financed by Tony Wilson, New Order and Factory Records. It had only been open less than a year when we graced the stage. I'd frequented the place quite a lot and had never once seen it full. If there was thirty or forty people in there, it was a busy night. It was said the club lost money every year for the first five years of its existence.

It was, naturally, Morrissey who came up with the idea of adding flowers to the stage for that first time we played in February. It had such a cold, sterile, dark atmosphere that the addition of some flora could only brighten proceedings. At first, it was just a bunch. But by the time we did our third and final show of the year in November, we were *drowning* in flowers. But, of course, by then it was already established as Morrissey's visual identity.

Our first show there was only our third-ever gig. We supported another Manchester band, a jazz-funk outfit called 52nd Street who were signed to Factory. An unlikely pairing, I know. We were billed as 'Smiths' on the poster. The first thing Morrissey said when we took to the stage was, 'We are *The Smiths*, not Smiths. "These Things Take Time",' announcing the cue for us to launch into our first track. When we finished the first song, there was the sound of one person clapping – Cath Berry. She was the sister of Andrew Berry, our mate and, more importantly, our hairdresser.

Andrew was in the year above me at my all-boys' school. I first met him during a mid-'70s production of *Iolanthe*. We were also in another Gilbert and Sullivan operetta together, *HMS Pinafore*. A lot of sailors and lads in drag. Typical all-boys' school.

Some of the kids – yes, even me – had briefcases for holding all their school supplies. This look was not considered for one second by Andrew. Even at this young age, he was stylish. He had a canvas record bag with badges all over it that rested on his hip. He had an easy nonchalance about him. He gave off that feeling of, 'I know things that you don't' – about music; about the *real* world.

After we left school and the Smiths started, he used to hang around with Johnny a lot. They even shared a rented house for a while that belonged to Joe Moss. They'd DJ together at places like Berlin and Exit – a couple of clubs in Manchester. But he would also DJ at the Haç. The latest electro, Bobby O records, great disco cuts. Then, of course, he became a hairdresser and used to cut our hair. We didn't trust anybody else to touch a follicle on our heads. He knew what he was doing. He was styling it, making sure it was right. To him, it was a real art form. He even set up a salon in the basement of the Haçienda where we used to go and hang out often. He was a good mate of the band and part of the crew. It was Andrew who had helped persuade the promoters of the Ritz to let the Smiths play before Blue Rondo à La Turk the previous year. He just knew everyone.

Me and Andrew Berry. The only man we trusted to cut our hair!
© Peter Hope

Besides Andrew, another omnipresent character at the Haçienda was a French videographer named Claude Bessy. His company was called Icon Video, although his official title was the Haçienda's 'visual jockey'. He mostly shot the bands that were on Factory Records, but we were lucky enough that he also captured some great footage of our Haçienda shows.

Claude was very intense and uptight all the time. He'd lived an astonishing life: kicked out of the Sorbonne in Paris for showing up drunk and threatening a teacher; time as a hash dealer in Afghanistan; prime mover in the LA punk scene of the mid-'70s before he ended up in Manchester in 1982. I do not think I ever saw him standing still. And you never saw him just walking anywhere. He was always rushing to get that perfect shot. He even ended up with his own Factory Records catalogue number for a video collection of his released in 1984, 'Bessy Talks Turkey'.

Claude always seemed to be frustrated, shouting at everyone and everything. He was so demanding. Everything had to be just so, to his specific taste. But he had an intensity about him that was weirdly infectious. I only exchanged words with him on a few occasions. However, when I did speak to him, his very demeanour just made me nervous. But I'm glad that he was around, because due to Claude filming that first February show, we have the only known footage of Johnny ever singing backing vocals live.

The second time we gigged at the Haç was 6 July 1983. Only five months had passed since we last played there, but due to how fast everything around the band was happening, it felt like an age. We'd got signed. We'd released our debut single. We'd survived Cannock Chase. It was also the biggest gig we'd played in our hometown, a fact not lost on Morrissey whose exuberance in front of an audience was growing with each show. 'Hello, you little charmers, we're the Smiths. How do you do?' he greeted the crowd.

The third and final time we played the club was on 24 November 1983, the same evening we were booked to play *Top of The Pops*. Our second single 'This Charming Man' had entered the UK top forty a couple of weeks earlier at number thirty-two – one place below the new offering from the Thompson Twins but ninety-two places higher than the peak of our previous, debut single. And as the single had risen two whole places in its second week on sale, the BBC deemed us show-worthy. This was huge.

We'd made our TV debut three weeks earlier on Channel 4's *The Tube* but only with a cheaply shot pre-record of us performing the single. *Top of the Pops* was the big one. The only problem was it was being broadcast live so we would appear on the show then jump on the train back up to Manchester and head straight onto the stage at the Haçienda later that night. We had toyed with getting a helicopter back up to Manchester, but this was quickly nixed due to Morrissey's fear of flying. I was a bit disappointed by that. Flying in helicopters seemed like what proper pop stars did.

When the decision was taken to do both *Top of the Pops* and play the Haçienda, I decided to ring a girl called Tina that I'd gone out with a while back. Believe it or not, this was the same girl that I had spied in the crowd at the Cyprus Tavern back when I had played there with the Hoax. When she asked me what I was up to, I casually mentioned that we were appearing on *Top of the Pops* as our first hit single 'This Charming Man' was in the charts and then we would be travelling straight up to Manchester to play a sold-out show at the Haçienda. I chanced my arm and asked her if she fancied coming to the show. 'No thanks, I've got plans, but hope it goes well,' came her ice-cold reply. I would need to try harder.

Hanging around the BBC Television Centre studio as we waited to perform for *Top of the Pops*, two girls walked over to us. They asked me if I was in a band. 'Yeah, we're in a band called the Smiths.'

They replied, 'Are you going to be playing?'

I smiled, 'Yeah, we've got to go on now actually.'

One of them replied in disbelief, 'Aren't you going to get changed? Surely you are not going on TV dressed *like that*, are you?' They were aghast. We were wearing jeans and crew-neck jumpers. Morrissey, more flamboyantly of course, was in a light turquoise oversized blouse, festooned with beads and clutching a giant bunch of gladioli. Floral accompaniment had become an integral part of Morrissey's stage performance since that Haçienda show earlier in the year, but *Top of the Pops* would not only introduce the band to most of the UK for the first time, but instantly cement the image of Mozzer as the flower-twirling frontman in the minds of the public for years to come.

Paul Young was on the same show performing his soon-to-be Christmas number two hit 'Love of the Common People' (despite 'This Charming Man' peaking at number twenty-five the following week, we were long gone by Christmas week). His guitarist seemed to have decided the best way to celebrate such chart success was to don an enormous box jacket. He was so over-shoulder-padded, he couldn't actually get through the door straight on, so he had to turn slightly sideways and scuttle through. We just looked at each other and sniggered.

In our minds, creating music did not equate with dressing up like you were in panto. We'd known some of the New Romantic crowd in Manchester, but we were always dress down as opposed to dress up. You don't *need* to wear ridiculous clothes. But of course many did. When we played 'Hand in Glove' with Sandie Shaw on *Top of the Pops* on 26 April 1984, six months after our first performance, Duran Duran were on the show too. We spoke to them briefly. They were dressed to impress. Before it was our turn to perform, I nipped to the toilet and into a cubicle that one of the band had just vacated. I was immediately hit by an almighty stink that took my breath away. It was completely at odds with their pomped and perfumed appearance. But they were very sweet to be fair – in conversation at least! They looked at us and we looked them up and down, each one of us individually thinking, *Well, I'm glad we didn't dress like that*. They knew we thought they looked ridiculous. And they knew we knew they knew. And vice versa.

Back at our debut performance in November '83, we were eventually told to take our positions as the live broadcast was about to start. Even though we were miming, I was still a bit jittery – this was *Top of the Pops*, for God's sake!

After we were introduced by Richard Skinner and teed up by fellow jock Simon Bates ('...and talking of charming men, at number thirty this week, these are the Smiths'), we were off. There was no time for any further jitters. I was playing away, trying to concentrate and there were balloons being knocked about *everywhere*. The audience was told to make it a party atmosphere, regardless of what band was on or what music they were playing. Somebody had hit a balloon onto the stage. It went over Morrissey's shoulder and started coming towards me. I was so anxious about doing anything wrong. It slowly floated down, catching me in its crosshairs before finally coming to nestle insistently between my legs. Instead of just knocking it out of the way, I didn't do anything. I was so petrified about dropping a stick in front of 15 million viewers all watching our first live TV performance.

We played the show nine times in all, our last performance more than three years later with 'Sheila Take a Bow' and it was never without incident, be that regular debasement at the hands of the BBC make-up girls, Killing Joke – who I loved – sneering at us like a bunch of ageing school bullies or Morrissey finding himself deep in conversation at the BBC bar with topless model and part-time pop star Samantha Fox, earnestly discussing the pros and cons of various hairspray brands.

By the time we got back to Manchester that evening, it was late. But after the empty, echoing Haçienda on our first outing, we were thrilled that the gig was sold out. 1,500 people! A disheartened queue of punters who *couldn't* get in snaked down Whitworth Street. We met Tony Wilson backstage who was noticeably excited at the atmosphere in the club.

He'd never seen anything like it he said. And considering unsavoury comedian Bernard Manning was booked to open the club eighteen months earlier and it had been losing money ever since, I imagine Tony meant it.

When we finally took to the stage, the first thing I noticed was the overpowering fragrance from all the flowers that we'd had shipped in to dress the place – as well as those the fans had brought along themselves. And, secondly, the crowd went berserk from the very first song to the last. At times it got quite hairy. It looked like people were getting injured in the frenzied melee. The following week, *Melody Maker* reported that 'even before they took the stage, girls were being pulled aside for treatment after fainting and too much screaming'. We played two encores, performing both 'This Charming Man' and 'Hand in Glove' for a second time in the set. We'd come a long way from Cath Berry clapping alone in February.

26

ENGLISHMEN IN NEW YORK

In December 1983, we had our very first dates in the US, starting in Manhattan and then across the Hudson to New Jersey and on to Boston. The only experience I'd had of America was through the television. Of course, TV programmes provided a warped version of the real thing, but New York, it turns out, *was* weird. It felt dangerous and edgy. Which it probably was. It was a good ten years before the big clean-up and gentrification. Like all first-time tourists, the little things seemed exotic to us. But who *hasn't* gone to New York for the first time and been excited like a small child to see the steam pouring out from the manholes? All of our senses were assaulted. It was overwhelming. I didn't really understand the place and the place was certainly struggling to understand me and the rest of the crew.

We stayed in the Iroquois Hotel on West 44th Street. Check out the online reviews nowadays and you'll be promised 'an upscale urban retreat blending modern luxury with classic New York charm'. But back then it was a shithole, with the obligatory cockroaches sharing our accommodation and a tiny window overlooking the view of a brick wall, just like on the TV. It was very dark and extremely claustrophobic. Of course, this was the *real* New York, but I think we all would have been happier staying somewhere completely fake. In 1983, people didn't go to New York for a

```
83-12-20  18:12
Msg 695 Title : SMITHS

THE SMITHS  : NEW YORK DECEMBER/JANUARY 1984.
-------------------------------------------------
RESPONSIBLE AGENT IN U.S.A.:RUTH POLSKI,BLIND DATES,90 WEST HOUSTON
-----------------------------------
                    ST,10R,NEW YORK CITY,NY10012.TEL:(212)260-4921.
FLIGHTS:
--------
29TH DECEMBER.
--------------
FLIGHT TW701 DEPARTS LONDON HEATHROW AIRPORT TERMINAL 3 AT 1345 AND
ARRIVES J.F.K. NEW YORK AT 1625.
RUTH POLSKI WILL MEET YOU AT THE AIRPORT AND TAKE TO HOTEL.

9TH JANUARY.
------------
FLIGHT TW704 DEPARTS J,F,K,NEW YORK TWA TERMINAL AT 2100 AND ARRIVES
LONDON HEATHROW TERMINAL 3 AT 0840 ON 10TH JANUARY.

HOTEL:
------
IROQUOIS HOTEL,49 WEST 44TH STREET,NEW YORK CITY,NY 10019.
TEL:(212)840-3080/1.
2 X 3 AND 1 SINGLE.

TEMPERATURE:
------------
BE PREPARED IT WILL BE VERY COLD,APPROX 20 DEGREES FAHRENHEIT.

SEND US A POSTCARD AND BUY SOME NICE HATS IN PHILADELPHIA..........
```

Telegram from our US tour organiser sent just before we
made our first trip to the States in December 1983.

holiday. They didn't travel from thousands of miles for the theatres, the museums or a spot of weekend shopping. They travelled there for work. People got *out* of New York, if they were lucky enough to be able to afford to do so. Only the hardcore remained.

The first thing I wanted to eat when I got there was an authentic, fresh New York pizza. Bear in mind, Pizza Hut restaurants in the UK were still a bit of a rarity in 1983 and all you got in the supermarket were those horrible frozen things. I approached the counter and launched into my politest Queen's English, 'Hello Sir, may I please have a pizza with cheese and tomato on it?'

'Cheese and *tom-ar-do?*', the dude mocks me with a particularly bad attempt at an English accent. '*Tom-ar-do?!*' he repeats for unnecessary emphasis.

158

He twists around to face the other men leaning against the ovens in the back of the shop.

'This guy just asked for cheese and *tom-ar-do*!' The entire crew starts cackling. He looks back to me and says derisively, 'Hey buddy, *every* pizza has cheese and *tom-ar-do*.'

We got the piss taken out of us wherever we went. The same thing happened at another restaurant when I asked for butter to go with my bread. '*Bud-ha?* What is "*budha*", my friend?' a boggled waiter enquired. We were always fair game.

We played at the notorious Danceteria in New York on New Year's Eve 1983. It was our first US concert and the first time we had played outside Ireland or the UK. Playing before us for about twenty minutes or so was the club's former coat-check girl. She'd recently released her debut album in the US and was actually promoting the single 'Holiday', which broke her worldwide the following year. The artist was called Madonna. Funnily enough, the previous year she'd supported our hometown contemporaries A Certain Ratio at the same club.

Tickets were priced at $20 in advance and $25 at the door, which seems extortionate now, but this was New York on New Year's Eve. In the backstage area of the club, there was a couch that me, Johnny and Andy were sitting on, trying to take it all in. It was quite obvious that cocaine was the drug of choice – and not ecstasy at that point, which some people think – and it was being taken quite openly, which wasn't normal behaviour where we came from.

Nothing felt real. It was like being on a film set. The black walls were covered in graffiti, the floor was concrete, there was a guy in drag on the door who directed you to an old-fashioned lift with sliding iron gates, and all the while everyone around us was overtly hoovering white powder up their noses. It only served to reinforce the fact that we were in a foreign land a long way from home.

But whatever our cultural differences, when we finally went on after

159

midnight, we were embraced by the hip New York revellers. And this was without them really knowing any of our songs. Despite his desire to sign us on the spot at our London ICA show in October, it was not until that trip to New York that the deal was agreed with Seymour Stein to officially license the Smiths from Rough Trade. But then, halfway through our seven-song set, Morrissey vanished. He took a tumble off the chest-high stage and disappeared out of sight. We continued playing as our singer recovered, reappeared and didn't miss a single line. Was he hurt? Not physically, I don't think. Adrenaline is a powerful anaesthetic. But his pride? Absolutely. Falling over is always a bit embarrassing. But on stage at your very first American show with everything else about your carefully cultivated, public-facing persona under your control? Well, that's on another level.

A similar thing happened to me a couple years later at a gig in Dublin. As I stepped off a three-foot-high drum riser, my foot got caught in a light cable and I fell forward. It wasn't a flat fall either; it was a 45-degree plunge, with my face taking the impact.

Johnny's amp was on the riser with a reverb plate. The sound the amp made when I hit the ground was *massive*, echoing around the hall. The crowd gasped thinking the sonic BOOM was the sound of my face hitting the floor. It was just the amp's reverb unit reacting. But I remember lying there thinking, *Am I hurt? Do I stay down*, pretend *to be hurt and wait for someone, or do I get up and risk looking like a dick?* I decided to go for the dick option.

After New Year's Eve at the Danceteria, we were scheduled to play City Gardens in New Jersey on 6 January. However, I woke up the morning we were due to leave and felt absolutely shocking. I called Johnny and Andy and said, 'Can you come to my room? I really don't feel very good.' I prised myself out of bed and crept to the bathroom. I didn't recognise my own reflection in the mirror. Bright red spots inflamed and mocked my face. I opened my eyes wide and they were shrouded with huge, red bumps. I had them on my tongue. I checked the rest of my body; I was covered.

The boys finally arrived. I was back in bed, with the lights off.

'What's wrong?' they asked. I switched on the overhead lamp. 'Have a look at this.'

They took one look at me and both shouted, 'Oh my God!' in perfect, almost comical unison and ran out, slamming the door behind them. I could hear Andy bellowing, 'You're going to die!' as they sprinted away down the hall. It wasn't the reassurance I had been looking for.

It transpired that I wasn't going to die but did have a particularly nasty bout of the chicken pox. Our other two US dates were cancelled.

PART 4

HOW SOON IS CELEBRITY?

27

BAND LIFE

1984

When we got back from the US, Morrissey and I were sat in my car and he showed me the picture that was going to be used as the cover art for our forthcoming debut album. It was a promotional still taken from Andy Warhol's 1968 movie *Flesh*, starring Joe Dallesandro as a hustler working in New York City. It's an image of two young men on a bed, Dallesandro is looking down at his crotch, while the other – Louis Waldon – leers at him and licks his lips in what can only be deduced as anticipation. I was pretty shocked. Of course, Morrissey showed me this full version, which is far more explicit than the cropped close-up that became the final cover. He didn't tell me that it was going to be trimmed down; I think he was trying to test me, to see if I'd say, 'I'm not fucking playing on *that*,' but I just shrugged it off. 'Yeah, cool' was my response.

The picture was homoerotic, but the image wasn't overtly sexual. It wasn't like the Stones' *Sticky Fingers* with a pair of jeans and the guy's fucking knob bulging through the denim. The photo was alluding to something without blatantly showing anything. But I think it's only really 'Hand in Glove' and *The Smiths* that had that similar homoeroticism. I think if I had felt strongly about the way we were at times presenting our art – that sexual ambiguity, the element of queerness – I would have said so from the outset. Besides, we were also signed to a label called 'Rough Trade' for fuck's sake. I thought it was important to be ruffling a few feathers.

I then had to show it to my parents, two people whose feathers I didn't *want* to ruffle. They were proud as punch that I was in a proper band with gigs and records and *Top of the Pops*, so I wasn't thinking, *Oh my God, what will their reaction be when they see the full album cover photo?* Of course, when they first saw the image it was the edited album cover. But neither of them batted an eyelid. Live and let live. I loved my parents for that.

At this point, we still weren't that famous; the Smiths was just a band that I was in. Morrissey was just a lad from Stretford, who most people still called Steve. In those early days, this wasn't the guy in the public domain who had recently and rather emphatically become MORRISSEY. That level of self-importance and notoriety came later, but when the album was released in February 1984, things changed. On its release, it went straight into the British charts at number two. Not the indie chart, the *actual* chart. It was only held off the top spot by the Thompson Twins. We had never dreamed that this was in any way possible. At the time, all four of us were incredibly proud of how the songs sounded even before we'd recorded the album, and we knew the album was good, but there are loads of bands that think what they have created is a masterpiece, only for their cherished release to fade into obscurity. Well, that didn't happen with our baby. The album would remain in the charts for thirty-three weeks – such an unbelievable result.

X

Around this time, something happened that challenged the bond we had forged as a band. The dynamic shifted from the four wide-eyed inno-cents shuffling around New York as a gang, taking on the world together, to the Smiths being a *business venture* with each individual looking out for themselves. There's that old quote about the pram in the hallway being the enemy of art. Well, I think an accountant or manager can have the same effect with friendships, especially when you still don't have an official manager.

In early 1984, we had a meeting with the accountancy firm Arthur Young, McLelland, Moores & Co in London.

All four of us went to the meeting: me, Andy, Johnny and Morrissey. I did not know who was responsible for arranging the gathering and had even less of an idea as to what was going to be discussed.

As far as I was concerned, all accountants did was your *accounts*. I didn't really understand the point of the meeting. In my naïvety, I didn't realise that there was a lot of moving finances around to get the best tax returns, that there was a plan to 'manage our money', to make it *work* for *us. Can't our accountants just take care of this? Isn't this what we paid them to do?* That was what I was thinking. It felt like we were there out of courtesy. It was, I hate to say it now, a bit boring.

There were a number of issues that were brought up. After a pregnant silence, the accountant looked at me and Andy pointedly and proclaimed, 'Obviously, a subject that we need to discuss is that when the Smiths split up, you can't expect to receive recording royalties indefinitely.'

I was completely blind-sided. '*Really?*' I questioned.

'Well, there *has* to be a cut-off point. You can't expect to receive royalties in perpetuity.'

'I didn't even know that was a thing that could be *changed*,' I responded.

I looked at Morrissey and Johnny for a reaction.

But neither of them said anything. They just both stared at the floor and looked a bit sheepish.

Hold on a minute, I thought. *Why are the accountants only looking at me and Andy?*

I spoke up, even though my bandmates remained silent. I really needed to understand.

'I'm not sure about that at all. I don't think that's something that I've ever heard of before today ... and it's not something that we should pursue.' The first thing I thought afterwards was, *Well, where would it go? You know, if our royalties don't carry on coming to us, where would they go instead?*

The subject of the band splitting up just as we were starting to garner some success seemed like a really odd thing to discuss. I never considered we'd be essentially strong-armed into trying to sign *a pre-nup* – if I'd even known what that was back then! It just seemed ridiculous. I mean, why were we even talking about when the band was going to split up? We were only just getting going.

The accountants moved the meeting on to other matters and the subject of royalty payments potentially not being made to Andy and myself was dropped. The topic was never spoken of ever again.

X

We were on the road for the whole of 1984 in support of the release of *The Smiths* – more than sixty-five shows, the bulk of which occurred in the first half of the year. We played a set of shows in Scotland that March. The gig in the Queen Margaret Union in Glasgow on the 2nd was overheated, overcrowded and, most likely, oversold. Fans were passing out. But it was an incredible gig, with a lot of enthusiastic heckling from the crowd who Morrissey playfully chastised. The next night, we were at the Dundee University Students' Union. Further bolstering his theatrical frontman persona, Morrissey shared grapes with fans, kissed another on the cheek and clapped back at hecklers after being showered in an almost constant deluge of warm lager from air-bound beakers. It felt like a defining moment for us, such was the fervour and devotion from the

Voice and The drums, 1983.
© Martin Joyce

usually locally partisan Scottish crowd. The world was less connected in those days, but the shared passions people did have – record shops, weekly music papers, John Peel – were shared and loved by *millions*. We would have got nowhere without their blessing.

June 1984 found us back in London, this time as part of the line-up for council leader Ken Livingstone's Jobs for a Change concert. Organised by the Greater London Council (GLC), the free festival was designed to promote employment 'awareness' and took place on the South Bank. The main stage – on which we played – was actually set up in the car park in the shadow of the splendour of County Hall. Estimates put the total crowd attending the event at about 150,000 people.

Also on the eclectic bill were Billy Bragg, Aswad, Misty in Roots, Mari Wilson, Ivor Cutler, Gil Scott-Heron and, perhaps most incongruously, the Flying Pickets, famous for the previous year's Christmas number one – an a cappella version of Yazoo's 'Only You'.

Livingstone introduced us with a fine balance of crowd flattery and band-approved understatement: 'I have walked through this car park every day for the last five years and it's never looked as good as it does now. The Smiths.'

By the time we went back on for our second encore, Morrissey was leading the 50,000-strong crowd gathered to see us in shouts of 'Smiths! Smiths! Smiths!' before finishing with 'Pretty Girls Make Graves' and 'Miserable Lie'.

About two weeks later on 23 June, we made our first – and last – appearance at Glastonbury. Or the 'Glastonbury CND Festival' as it was then known. Elvis Costello was headlining on the Saturday we were playing, and acts as disparate as Ian Dury, Fela Kuti, Weather Report and Joan Baez were featured across the rest of the three-day event. A weekend ticket for Glastonbury nowadays will set you back in the region of £355. In 1984, it was £13.

We arrived on site, spilling out of our battered old nine-seater Mercedes. The trusty blue Renault Master was no more and the Merc had become our new mode of transport. We took whatever gear we could fit in the car with us and the rest followed behind us in a van.

Originally due on at 6 p.m., we had been bumped back due to one of the earlier bands, Amazulu, arriving late and missing their slot. Nowadays they would have been told to sod off, but back then, in the days before tight BBC scheduling and the slick corporatisation of the event, they were given a free pass by the far more relaxed hippies who ran the show and still held sway. Besides, Amazulu had featured as one of the weekly musical turns on the seminal anarchic comedy *The Young Ones* earlier in the month. Their credit was good. Irrespective, we were going on late.

You are always faced with the same two risks at any festival: the weather and the crowd. Down the years, the success of any Glastonbury has been judged by the amount of rain that fell before or during the event.

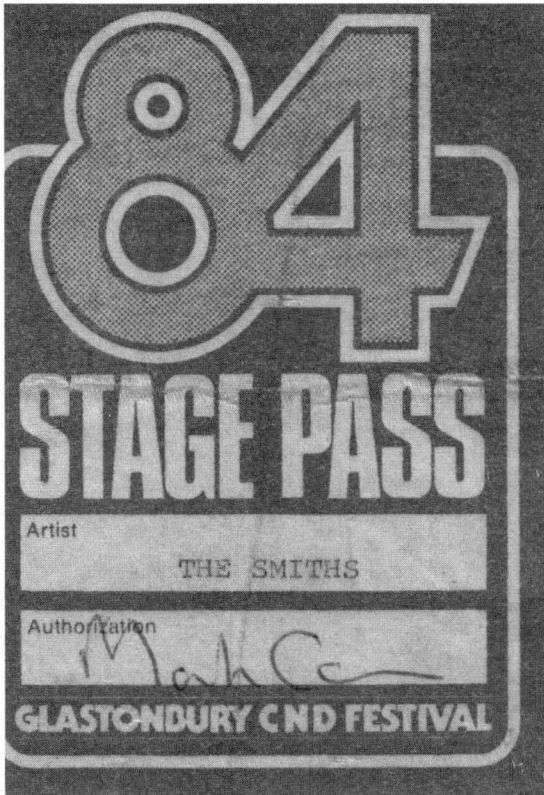

Backstage pass for the 'Glastonbury CND Festival' as it was then known, 1984.

Was it a dry one or was it a mud bath? Thankfully, our experience was positive. The second risk was the crowd. Given the nature of the festival, you're not playing to your crowd *per se*. You have to work that bit harder to win over a less devoted audience. And to do that, you've got to sound good. And this is where our problems started. So, as we tore into our first number 'Nowhere Fast' – an unreleased song opening a festival, a bold decision – the first thing I noticed was just how terrible the drums sounded. And it wasn't just me. Both Johnny's guitar and Morrissey's vocals were coming through the bass amp. Andy's bass was ... well, fuck knows. We were on the Glastonbury Pyramid Stage, the weather was good and we sounded shit.

The effect was just *thin*. I was used to the drums sounding big, fat, heavy and powerful. And here they just sounded like a children's drum kit, tinny and ineffective. Also, I was so far away from the PA, which didn't help. The monitors I was given were woefully inadequate. Pretty much every gig we'd played up until then was indoors and a lot smaller. We'd just played the GLC, which was also open air, but on a much smaller stage, more contained with a lower cover above the stage. Glastonbury's stage was immense. The sound was fucked.

The fact that you don't have a soundcheck at Glastonbury, or indeed any festival, is a massive pain in the arse. You just go on and play. And hope for the best. They do a line check to make sure everything's working, and a mic check, just to make sure there is sound out front, but you don't really get a *feel* for the place. Normally, you go into a venue in the afternoon, you set up, have a play, ask the sound guy to do this or that. At least in those scenarios you know what you're dealing with before you start playing in front of an audience; processing everything that sounds wrong in real time in front of 30,000 people. I might even have got used to it, rather than walking off stage and thinking, *Oh God, what was that?!*

We got the *curly finger* to come off after less than half an hour. We hadn't come close to finishing the set. Ten short songs. And the sound team had just started to fix the problem. We were paying the price for the earlier Amazulu accommodation. Even though it was much shorter than our usual performances, pockets of fans in the crowd were still trying to get on stage. I think Johnny even helped the first fan up himself, which didn't go down too well. This wasn't something that usually happened at Glastonbury. I don't think they had stage invasions. To discourage people, the festival had put oil on a corrugated iron ramp at a 45-degree angle to stop people from getting up on stage, but our fans managed anyway. They were tenacious fuckers. Security was stomping on their hands to get them off. It was a bit chaotic – not *quite* a riot – but not an afternoon picnic.

When we cut the set short, a dark mood started to emanate from the crowd. People were annoyed because they thought we hadn't played long enough. Things were thrown, there was a noticeable rising tide of jeers and whistles. But it wasn't our fault. We had no control over our early exit. It was a baptism of fire.

Ironically, when Glastonbury founder Michael Eavis was asked what his favourite gig was out of the tens of thousands of incredible artists who've played at Glastonbury over its six-decade history, he said the Smiths. Despite his initial frustration with the sound, even Johnny came to admire our performance, stating it was an important moment in getting to hear and see quite how *unusual* our songs sounded when you heard them wrenched from their usual hermetic context. He liked it. I think we all did. Eavis apparently considered our appearance to be a seminal moment in the history of the festival and a turning point in the way that Glastonbury was viewed. Glastonbury back then was very different from the festival it is today. It might take a few more years to fully reach maturity, but we'd helped plant some new seeds. And if anyone was going to understand that, it was surely going to be a farmer.

X

We returned to London in July, this time to record at Jam Studios in north London. Johnny had been working on the riff for a tune that had the working title of 'Swamp'. It was the rudimentary start of what would become 'How Soon is Now?'. To give you some idea of just how on fire Johnny was at this point, 'Swamp' was conceived over the same four-day period in June when he also wrote 'William, It Was Really Nothing' and 'Please, Please, Please Let Me Get What I Want'. Quite mind-blowing. John Porter was back as producer. The method in the studio was to record all the parts live, keep the drums, overdub the bass and then work on the guitars. And I mean, *really* work. We would have the rhythm section

173

wrapped, then Johnny would put his main guitar part down and another and another and another ... there's something like thirteen guitars on 'How Soon is Now?'.

When we recorded that track, with the exception of Moz, of course, we all got *really* stoned. We took all of the regular bulbs out of the light fittings and replaced them with red ones, so it was a bit like a dark room. We created this smoky, trippy atmosphere. We wanted the mood to feel as though we were being pulled under by quicksand.

The working relationship between Johnny and John was at its strongest during the recording of 'How Soon is Now?'. They were putting in long hours and coming up with some incredible ideas together. Unfortunately, I think the same issues as before still existed between John and Morrissey. He would record his vocal but, again, there was no guidance up top and little in the way of feedback or reassurance afterwards. Instead, John would merely react in closed questions – 'Are you happy with that? Would you like to do it again?' Looking for some sort of musical counsel or affirmation, Morrissey could only reply with his own canvassing in return; 'Well, do you *think* I need to do it again?' They never found a constructive way to communicate.

Anyone not being able to operate on the same wavelength as Morrissey and accommodate his standards and expectations would never last long around us. Some people would point-blank refuse and were quickly out of the door. Others would attempt to adapt through gritted teeth and that didn't end well for them either. Everyone had to be comfortable rubbing along with the grain to create the right environment. If not, Morrissey couldn't relax. And none of us could. So with that in mind, was there a particular attitude you would need to adopt around Mozzer in order *make* him feel comfortable? I don't think so. It really was as simple as 'If he liked you, he liked you.' He didn't pretend to like someone if he didn't, because he never believed he *had* to. Why waste everyone's time? Even in that working

174

environment where you are more tolerant of other's differences in order to achieve a shared goal? He wouldn't do that either. There's a very good reason why so many people outside of the band have found it so hard to work with him.

But the idea of having somebody around us who was '*non*-Smiths' in outlook and attitude was a tall order for any of us to accept. I think that's one of the reasons why we all struggled with management. As I've said before, the magic was in the dynamic of the four of us. John Porter was dismissed after we finished 'Nowhere Fast' and 'How Soon is Now?'. The next album would be recorded by the Smiths and produced by the Smiths.

28

MAKING
MEAT IS MURDER

Tina and me around the time that we moved down to London.

Over the spring of 1984, all four of us moved to London from Manchester, bedding down in various areas of the city. It seemed the right thing to do as everything involving the music industry was based in the Big Smoke. Johnny got a place in Earl's Court: quite a vibrant area in the early '80s, but it still felt a bit seedy. Morrissey was in Kensington: very plush and expensive. Andy and I decided that we would shack up with our mate Phil Powell in Willesden. Phil was working for the Smiths as a guitar tech and crew member, but his relationship with the band was so tight that he was virtually a member. By this time, Tina and I had been together for a while and she had agreed to join me.

A few months back, after eventually convincing Tina to go on some dates with me, I was invited round to her parents', the Rileys, for a meal. I remember feeling nervous, but I had nothing to fear as Tina's mum was a lovely lady who welcomed me in with a motherly warmth. Apparently, I arrived dressed to impress with some New Romantic-style winkle pickers on. Decades later, Tina's mum would enjoy reminding me about how that night my shoes entered the house followed by me ten minutes later.

Tina's dad was another prospect altogether. This was an educated guy who had worked as an engineer at a place called Mirlees on the manufacturing of steam engines. He would later become a teacher in English, maths and the sciences. I was pretty sure they both hoped for someone better for their precious daughter – a doctor or a solicitor maybe – not the scruffy punk that arrived at the house in his foot-long winkle pickers.

Almost immediately upon arrival, I realised that this was going to be a very different experience to dining at the Joyce household. For a start, everyone sat down at the table. At home in Wilbraham Road, the table was parallel with your knees, sitting on the sofa. I also noticed the Rileys had some strange items on their dinner table. There, above where the knife and fork were set, was a spoon. I had no idea what it was for. After we'd finished the main meal, a dessert was brought out which

178

Me at the Rileys' house. Note the dessert spoon!

was pineapple tart with custard, if I remember correctly. I finally realised what the spoon was for.

Before making the move to London, I decided to speak to Tina's dad, John. John was a little old-fashioned, so I wanted to have a chat with him as I thought he would appreciate me coming to him before the two of us took the step of moving in together down in London. I was a bit daunted at the conversation, but it turned out that he was only too happy for us to make the move and wished us the best of luck with it. I know it sounds outdated, but he was from a very different time and I thought it was right and proper for me to ask him.

Moving from Manchester to London in the early '80s was a big culture shock. Tina signed up with a temp agency and secured a job at the television company TV-am. TV-am broadcast the UK's first big commercial daily breakfast television show. Their studios were based in Camden, right on the Regent's Canal.

Tina worked with the presenters at TV-am. On the rare occasion when I would have time off, I'd meet her for lunch, often strolling from her office to Camden Market. There was always plenty to look at and admire, between the market's offerings of clothes and other random items. On one occasion, I noticed someone selling bootleg records at one of the stalls. As I was scanning what was on offer, I spied a copy of our Fall gig at the Electric Ballroom from the year before. I had to have it, but I was shocked when I saw it was priced at £15. I decided to try and bargain with the seller. 'Hi mate, you're not going to believe this, but I'm actually the drummer in the Smiths and I really want this. Can you give me a bit of a discount?' He looked at me with a deadpan expression and responded with no emotion. 'Absolutely not. In fact, that's been priced wrong. It's actually £25.' Unbelievable. Needless to say, I left empty-handed.

Willesden is very much pushing at the outer edges of Greater London, five miles from the centre of the city and, at the time, it was a bit run-down. All four of us shared one house, but it quickly became clear it wasn't working. The ZX Spectrum home computer had just come out, so me, Andy and Phil would stay up all night playing video games with poor Tina feeling a bit sidelined.

Tina and I managed to get a short break away at the start of the sweltering summer, shortly followed by Andy and Phil, who went off to do their own thing. When we arrived home, we heard this strange, insistent buzzing sound coming from the kitchen. I opened the door and the room was completely black with flies. The boys hadn't emptied the bin before they left and the place was infested. It was time for me and Tina to move out.

So we moved to Arkwright Road in Hampstead. It was a nicer place than the gaff in Willesden, but still a bit too far away from the action and the bright lights of the dream of London I'd been sold. It was pretty, leafy and very green, but it was still just a bedsit. A room with a kitchen and a bedroom. Tight quarters for sure.

The move down to the capital didn't last long for any of us and, later that year, we all ended up picking up again and going back to where we started, back to Manchester. It felt right to me. I always just felt a little bit like a fish out of water in London. I did – and still do – have a love/hate relationship with the place. But, fundamentally, Manchester is ultimately *home* for me and always will be. I've travelled the world and visited some astonishing places, but nothing really compares to the feeling I get when I return here. I couldn't put my finger on it forty years ago. I was young. Life seemed like a bigger adventure with the world waiting to be explored. But I also needed to feel grounded. We travelled all the time. Gigs. Recordings. Interviews. I needed the sanctuary that only Manchester has ever been able to offer me.

But I also think that once Morrissey had decided he wanted to move back – he was still dealing with the dilemma of trying to work out what he wanted and where he wanted it – it just felt natural for the rest of us to follow. We came down together, we went home together. In 1984, as everything was just starting to explode, that was really important to us.

X

After we moved back to Manchester, we started work on our second album, firstly at Amazon Studios in October before moving to Ridge Farm Studios in November. Amazon – which became Parr Street Studios in the early '90s – was located on an industrial estate in Kirkby, just outside Liverpool. Ridge Farm was a beautiful residential studio near Dorking in Surrey. Ironically, we'd just moved back up to Manchester and here we were, back in the south again. I love recording in a residential studio. There's no faffing about with cars or taxis. No wasting the morning getting your shit together before you eventually start recording at noon. Just wake up, have a nice, sociable, home-cooked breakfast together and crack on.

During the recording, I got myself a new drum kit: a beautiful Yamaha 9000 Recording Series in a cherry-red finish. I still have it. It's the kit I recorded everything on from that point. Johnny had encouraged me to purchase it, reminding me that the band account would pay for the cost of the kit that I had my eye on. It was one of the best things I ever did. I felt inspired. When I listen to that album now, I can still hear that excitement and immediacy in my playing.

We'd drive ourselves to Kirkby every day, all piled into the old Merc for the 30-mile trip down the M62. It was a bitterly cold winter and naturally one of our party pulled rank on always assuming the prime spot that best enjoyed the car's heater. But we'd arrive at Amazon feeling pretty focused on our intentions. We did three or maybe four backing tracks each day, which is pretty good going. There was a real energy to the sessions, a feeling that we'd managed to give the adults the slip and were now free-wheeling the ship alone. It was liberating.

Once you've had a hit, anything less than equalling that next time round is seen as a failure. It's stupid, of course, but as determined, competitive artists, we put these pressures on ourselves. I'm not sure we saw the Smiths as having any direct peers. We knew we were different and we knew we were special. The bar we aspired to was set by Bowie, the Stooges, the Beatles, Bolan, Chic, Elvis. In essence, we were only competing against ourselves. *The Smiths* had reached number two in the chart and gone platinum within a year. 300,000 copies sold. The next album might not be so big for many reasons – but going backwards at this point in our career would have felt like a disaster. But you're also dealing with second album syndrome. You have your whole career, your whole *life*, to draw on the material for your first album. And everyone knows the songs. You've been playing them live for years. But your second album? Twelve months. And then you've got the whole dilemma at what speed you progress. You've got to keep the original fans happy so you can't change direction too far, too soon. But equally you can't just rest on your laurels and repeat exactly the same formula – however successful – that worked first time round. It's an incredible burden to carry if you're the main songwriter.

But because Johnny was just *so* prolific and *so* confident in what he was writing, I really don't think he felt that pressure as much as possibly the rest of us did. If he did, he kept it quiet.

The songs just kept on coming.

Every time I'd see Johnny, whether it was in the studio, at sound-checks or just messing around in whatever down-time we had, he was always playing with a new riff.

And it was always moving quickly. Keep it fresh. 'That sounds great. Right, let's do that. Let's put that down.'

When we returned to the studio after parting ways with John Porter, we wanted to be able to fully realise our own vision. Johnny knew what he wanted musically – the sound of the Smiths in his head. But the logistical and practical side of a mixing desk – all the buttons, routing and EQ – was a whole new challenge.

The real issue was that none of us were trained audio engineers. A three-band EQ-standard equipment for home recording usually gives you control over treble, mid and bass. But in a professional studio, you might have a *thirty-one*-band EQ with detailed frequency control – and that's just one piece of a very complex puzzle. It's not just about pushing buttons. There are patch bays and multiple effects to be added to various instruments. Over time, engineers know how to do this intuitively. They've trained for this, put in the hard yards. There's a lot less sex and drugs and rock 'n' roll for engineers. Anybody else would have struggled to perform even the simplest task on a mixing desk. Me personally, I didn't have a clue. Not a fucking clue.

In short, we didn't want to have to spend hours learning the basics, let alone the intermediary and advanced levels of music engineering. We wanted to play, to create and to totally trust someone else to make it all sound great. That's the invaluable role of a great engineer.

Enter Stephen Street.

We had first encountered 'Streety', as we called him, when we were recording what would become our first top ten single 'Heaven Knows I'm Miserable Now' the previous year at Island Records' Fallout Shelter studio, which used to be housed in the basement of their headquarters in Hammersmith. John Porter was on production duties, with Stephen Street engineering the session. There's a pecking order in the studio: producer at the top, then engineer, tape operator and gopher (somebody you can ask to go and pick up any essentials you may require: strings, drumsticks, ciggies, tea, coffee). Stephen was smart and articulate, especially when he talked about what could or couldn't be achieved, what ideas may or may not work.

There was no hesitation or uncertainty – he just got on with it. Stephen had the ability of being able to process and respond instantly to creative ideas without slowing down the session. His experience allowed us to focus on performance and songwriting while he handled the technical side. We liked him immensely. He was a brilliant ally.

In the studio, I just tried to keep my head down and let things evolve naturally. There was always the risk of setting certain people off by saying the wrong thing. By definition of his role, Stephen was always more involved in the practical creative decisions but quickly learned never to be overbearing. It's a fine line. We were still at a point as a band where if you weren't an actual Smith, any person who proffered an unsolicited idea would be met with a withering glare.

But we weren't so cocky that we would overlook both the talents and the temperament of this pre-naturally gifted twenty-four-year-old. And this was important. The four of us were aged between twenty-one and twenty-six so we were contemporaries. This was something we couldn't quite share with John Porter, who, having been born in 1947, had felt far more teacherly in the dynamic adopted with us.

But despite his relative youth, Stephen was also very straight – completely drug-free, which we appreciated. It was like knowing the airline pilot hadn't had a few stiff ones before take-off. All those buttons and faders and dials and switches – we needed a safe and sober pair of hands in our own cockpit as well. Not that we were *wild* as such, but we did get stoned in the evenings (again, Moz excluded). Stephen might have a beer after hours, but he was always reassuringly sharp and clear-headed.

During one session at Amazon Studios, Streety went, 'Okay, onto the next track.'

Johnny turned to us and said, 'I've got this idea I've been working on for ages. Let's try it out.'

It was 'The Headmaster Ritual'. Although Johnny had it in his locker of songs, Andy and I hadn't really played it much at this point. So we just went through it, nodding when the breaks were and then we recorded it. Simple as that. This was one of the beauties of working with Johnny and Andy. There was this musical chemistry where Johnny would play a riff, Andy and I would play along and it would just sound great. We weren't purposely excluding Morrissey, but this was often how the guitar, bass and drums were put down. Obviously, Morrissey's voice is his instrument. But we never worked through songs in this way with Moz.

We didn't tell Stephen it was a track that we hadn't even practised properly, but he loved it. It had this urgency to it because we hadn't toured it and played it hundreds of times yet. When you're in a situation where you're recording a track that is relatively new, it adds a little excitement to the proceedings, which comes across in the urgency of the recording.

The night we finished laying down the track 'Meat is Murder', we all sat down for dinner together and started talking about vegetarianism. It would have been weird had it not come up. The words that Morrissey had provided for the track were some of the most powerful and heartfelt I'd ever heard. They were also totally unconventional for a pop song. He explained to me how he had stopped eating meat many years ago and he suggested I do the same. I said, 'Yeah, but the thing is, I don't eat any vegetables. I'm going to be screwed if I tried to live that way. I only eat meat and fish and chicken. If I don't eat meat, then I'll eat nothing.'

He tried a new tack. 'You're a cat lover, aren't you?' Morrissey knew full well that I had been a cat lover my whole life.

'Yeah.'

'Do you know what happens to pigs, sheep, cows and animals kept in farms?'

I didn't, but I had a pretty good idea.

'It's horrific,' he told me. 'The way that these animals are treated, the cruelty that's involved is off the scale. Would you do that to one of your cats? Would you treat them like that?'

'No, not at all, of course not.'

'Well, what's the difference between committing that kind of cruelty to a cat or a dog versus a pig or a cow?'

Honestly, I didn't have a good-enough answer. Initially, I was ready to defend my love for meat, prepared to argue the case. But, to my surprise, I found myself agreeing with him.

'You're right. I don't have an argument.' That was forty years ago. I've been a vegetarian ever since.

So, a 'pop song with unconventional lyrics'? Hardly. It was a whole manifesto.

It's easy to forget sometimes how 'cranky' you looked if you declared yourself a vegetarian in the first half of the 1980s. Look at the amount of stick Linda McCartney got. Yet, by 2024, her Linda McCartney vegetarian food business had a net worth of £250 million. Times change. In 1984 in the UK, it was estimated that 2 per cent of the population categorised themselves as vegetarian. By the end of 1985 – after *Meat is Murder* was released – that number had risen to 3 per cent, the equivalent of half a million people. Now, I'm not saying we were responsible for every single one of those conversions, but I *know* we played our part. We helped drive the conversation at a time when standing up for your beliefs, for animal rights, could be – and was – regularly mocked. And I'm incredibly proud of that.

But such a lifestyle change wasn't necessarily easy back then. Tina hesitantly agreed to join me and it was quite difficult at first, especially with the scarcity of choices when dining out. 'Vegetarian options' were, frankly, a load of shit back then. Restaurants at the time offered such wonderful, cutting-edge dishes that included chips, salad, mushrooms and eggs. And if it was a particularly gastronomic experience, the old nut roast. Excuse me while I lick my lips.

Touring in America wasn't much better. Although we were playing some pretty decent-sized venues, we didn't have the luxury of being able to bring our own catering with us. The in-house providers at the various places had been given a heads-up that what we required was simple fare. I remember in Dallas, we went up to where the food had been laid out for us. I got scrambled eggs and beans, then noticed these great big lumps dotted throughout in both dishes. 'What is that?', I asked, pointing to the strange gnarls in the baking pan. 'That is *seasonin'*,' the local caterers explained. I was not familiar with any herbs or spices that had gristle and bone attached to them and asked for further clarification as to what was swimming around in our food. 'Just some pig knuckles, used for seasonin',' they said. 'Pick 'em out if you don't want 'em.' As I moved along the queue, I heard one of the crew behind me ask for the steak. The woman who'd served me replied to his request in a voice loud enough for me to hear.

'At last! A *real* man!'

29

NO. 1

1985

Johnny and me, 1985.

A few months after finishing recording *Meat is Murder* in early 1985, I got a phone call out of the blue from Martha Defoe. Martha worked at Rough Trade and, despite not being a managerial employee, would more often than not perform unofficial managerial errands and tasks for the band and, in particular, Morrissey. She was one of his acolytes and became besotted with him. Nothing was too much trouble for her. Martha did not have any real authority to dictate any business dealings, but she completely bought into Morrissey's worldview. She was very well read and in many ways his intellectual equal. Because of her affinity to our lead singer, she became something of a spokesperson for him, seemingly regardless of how this might be seen by the rest of the band. Given how Morrissey was not the most effective communicator, Martha seemed to act as a conduit – articulating what he struggled to say. And she would often take the lead when it came to blunt conversations that Morrissey didn't want to instigate himself. Tact or diplomacy was never her strongest suit. Nor was it his.

On this particular occasion, she rang me to convey a message to me from our frontman.

'I've been speaking to Morrissey,' she said, 'and we think that your percentage should go down from a quarter share to 15 per cent.'

I was dumbfounded, '*Why?*' I asked.

'For a start, you're not doing any interviews,' she stated. 'Morrissey's writing the words to the songs.'

'Well, he's getting the publishing royalties for that,' I pointed out.

She continued to push her argument. 'Well, he's doing all the sleeves. He's not getting paid for that. He's doing all the interviews and not getting paid for that either.'

I said, 'Well, I'll do some of the interviews then.'

There was silence on the other end of the phone.

I continued. 'Look, the reason why he's doing all the interviews is he's so fucking brilliant at doing the interviews. He *wants* to do the interviews. He is every writer's dream. Whatever questions are thrown at him, he can deal with them perfectly. He knows what he's going to say before they've even asked him anything.'

She could not disagree.

Martha sighed, then answered, 'Well, it's something that we discussed.'

The discussion was irrelevant. 'Well, I'm not fucking having that wage cut. No chance.'

I put the phone down, called Morrissey straight away and told him clearly:

'There's no way I'm going to accept that idea. Are you mad?'

There was silence on the other end of the phone.

'You can't expect me to take less of a percentage because you do interviews! If you want me to do more interviews, I'll do more interviews, but you can't expect me to take a cut.'

Silence.

I battled on. 'Look, the sleeves are brilliant,' I conceded, 'and I accept that's something you're managing with Jo, but I can't and won't accept less money.'

Not a sound.

'You don't want to talk about this or even discuss it, do you?'

Nothing.

There was no reply, so there was nothing else to say.

I decided to draw a line under it, as the entire encounter was going nowhere.

'Okay, let's leave it then,' I finished before finally hanging up.

The subject was never revisited, and, as such, I assumed my percentage remained the same.*

When Morrissey couldn't tell someone difficult news, it wasn't out of laziness or arrogance. I just think he genuinely couldn't do it. I'd seen this before with him. It wasn't cowardice, it was almost like a physical block. It reminded me of soldiers in the First World War who froze in fear in the face of conflict. Some people are simply wired that way. I also think it's why he leant so heavily on his use of the fax machine or postcards and letters to friends – or enemies. It removed the need for any real face-to-face or verbal communication. He has a tolerance for the human race, which is complicated.

Morrissey was never part of a gang when he was growing up and I think that really showed. Johnny, Andy and I had all grown up in wide social circles with mates and girlfriends. Morrissey didn't have that. The band became his gang and when that dynamic was threatened in any way, he clung to it with everything he had, even if he came close to suffocating it. It wasn't just a career to him – it was salvation.

But that same fragility is why his lyrics have endured. They weren't crafted for effect; they were real. He wrote about feeling left out, about

---

* In March 1989, Mike began legal proceedings against Morrissey and Johnny Marr. He argued that he was entitled to a 25 per cent share of all non-songwriting profits based on the assertion that all four members were equal partners in the Smiths.

In December 1996, after acknowledgement from Morrissey and Johnny Marr that all four members were partners, the case reached the Chancery Division of the High Court of Justice. Acting on behalf of his client, Mike's barrister, Nigel Davis QC, stated that 'it was not until after the [bestselling] band split up in 1987 that his client discovered he was getting only 10 percent of the profits'.

After a week-long hearing at the High Court and based on the 1890 Partnership Act, the judge ruled in favour of Mike declaring that he was entitled to 25 per cent of profits with immediate effect, and a back payment of approximately £1 million was awarded. In late 1998, Morrissey staged an appeal that was rejected by the Court of Appeal.

not being able to go out, of standing at a club watching everyone else have fun while he felt miserable and alone.

People often say that talking through issues helps, that saying things out loud is a release. It is the same with Morrissey's lyrics. He didn't talk about these feelings openly – he sang them. He turned internal pain into something poetic and shared it with the world. And in doing so, he found his people who responded in more than kind. He found his *disciples*, both holding a mirror to each other.

Morrissey's on-stage persona was dramatic and theatrical, which was the opposite of his nature offstage. Like an actor putting on a mask stepping into a role, performance gave him permission to express things he couldn't say or do otherwise. Cutting all ties to the name, for 'Steven' to become 'Morrissey', was an act of reinvention.

The great character actor Peter Sellers once remarked 'I could never be myself. You see, there is no me, I do not exist.' It feels like the sort of sentiment that Morrissey could apply to himself. *Steven* no longer existed. To call Morrissey complex is an understatement. Yet he remains one of our truly great singers. His phrasing, his delivery and his emotional nuance are exceptional and there is a purity to his creative vision that is almost unparalleled.

X

On its release in February 1985, *Meat is Murder* entered the UK charts at number one. We had not only swerved the dreaded 'difficult second album' curse, we had knocked none other than *Born in the U.S.A.* by Bruce Springsteen off the top spot too. But relations with Rough Trade were starting to become strained.

Shortly after the release of the album, we were scheduled to perform on *Top of the Pops*. We arrived at the studio and were waiting to go on to record our track when there was a knock at the green room door. It was a courier with four large cardboard boxes. We opened them to reveal four gold discs commemorating 100,000 sales of *Meat is Murder*. Now, this was a massive achievement. A significant moment in any young musician's career. But the manner in which they had been presented to us felt like it was a bit of an inconvenient afterthought. No note, no card, no 'Well done, lads! With love from all of us at Rough Trade.' Less a big pat on the back and more a slap in the face. Not one soul from the record company was on hand to congratulate us. We wanted a bottle of bubbly, a snapper, a photo of four ecstatic faces that I could show my mum. Instead, what did we get to commemorate such an achievement? A plain brown box handed over by an anonymous messenger.

We were Rough Trade's first proper break-out success. Perhaps this was a world in which they were learning the ropes too? But worryingly, it all started to feel that a slight nonchalance, or perhaps a charming naïvety, was also disguising a lack of serious investment and promotion.

The reception and chart performance for *Murder* had been astonishing, but less than a month after it was released, our new standalone single 'Shakespeare's Sister' limped into the chart, peaking at number twenty-six. Three weeks later, it was gone completely. It was, as Morrissey later noted, released with 'a monstrous amount of defeatism' and did nothing to smooth our concerns. Our lack of management was proving to be increasingly problematic. Most other bands channelled their gripes through a trusted ally who only would act with the artists' best interests at heart. We were managing an increasingly fractious *business* relationship with Rough Trade by ourselves, while also trying to be the best fucking band in the country at the same time.

We went back out on the road touring to support *Meat is Murder* a little more than two weeks after its release. There were twenty-three dates that had been booked. I've still got a poster from that tour – put together by All Trade Booking – and in the corner it says: 'All dates completely sold out.' When the tour was originally conceived, those venues were probably the right size, but we'd already outgrown them by the time the shows happened.

Mike Hinc, who ran All Trade Booking, had a clear strategy. His thinking was that it was always better to have a 300-capacity venue packed with 200 people outside trying to get in than a 1,200-capacity place that's only half full. And so it was that, on 27 February 1985, the Smiths – at that point in time the hottest group in the country – opened the first night of their *Meat is Murder* tour in Chippenham.

Come April we were back in the capital for our second London date of the tour and our last UK date before we headed to Italy. We were playing the Royal Albert Hall.

We sold it out. With a capacity of 5,000, it was our biggest-ever show in London. But there was a musty, old-fashioned feel to the place, as if nothing had changed there for fifty years – even down to the old guy who knocked on our dressing room door dressed as Lurch from *The Addams Family*, who would periodically announce how long there was until show time: 'Excuse me, gentlemen! There are now *thirty* minutes until the show begins!' he would shout.

Pete Burns, lead singer of Dead or Alive, and the band's drummer Steve Coy joined us on stage for the first song of the second encore, 'Barbarism Begins at Home'. But what should have been a triumphant occasion all felt rather flat. It was in stark contrast to the Brixton Academy gig a month earlier which was *mayhem*! Fights in the audience, girls passing out... it was wild. Not our greatest-ever performance but certainly one of our most memorable. But I think the sound at the Albert Hall let us down and, given the distance between the crowd and the stage, it was hard for Morrissey to generate the sort of connection that he and the audience had been getting used to. He was uncharacteristically subdued throughout, even remarking before we started to play 'William...' that 'we probably picked the wrong venue'. I think he was right.

All things considered though, it had been a triumphant tour. Our next adventure on the road would prove to be more of a mixed bag. We were scheduled to play four dates in Europe. The first gig was in Rome at the Teatro Tendastrisce. Regrettably, it ended up being the only time we ever played live in Italy.* Though having been booked less than a week before our arrival, and with most of the communication taking place with the promoter Paolo Bedini via payphone, we filled the venue. Close to 4,000 punters. *Three* encores. It was a fantastic start to the European leg.

Three Spanish gigs were to follow in Barcelona, Madrid and San Sebastián. In Barcelona, we were booked to play at the venue Studio 54, which was an ersatz Spanish version of the legendary New York club of the same name, with a similarly mirrored disco aesthetic. Not *typically* Smiths. When we arrived in Madrid, we were informed that our show was actually a free concert financed by the city as part of the celebrations of its patron saint San Isidro. The Parque del Oeste on the Paseo de Camoens was a grassy open-air space, accommodating what was later reported to be tens of thousands of fans who had gathered to see us perform. The full show was filmed for cult Spanish TV programme *La Edad de Oro* and the eventual transmission was broadcast with a stilted interview between Johnny, Moz and the Spanish presenter, a translator in everyone's earpiece slowing down the regular ebb and flow of such occasions. On our UK tour the previous year, we'd starting using Prokofiev's 'Dance of the Knights' from his *Romeo and Juliet* ballet as our entrance music. We loved the power and the drama it lent the start of each gig, but it sounded particularly affecting in Madrid.

At the very start of the tour, the decision had been made to hire equipment instead of shipping out our own – drums, backline, everything

---

* We did play a huge indoor festival in Sanremo in 1987 that was televised. Our performance featured us miming to 'Shoplifters of the World Unite', 'Ask', 'The Boy With the Thorn in His Side', 'Panic' and 'There is a Light That Never Goes Out'.

– which would've cost a fortune. You never quite know what you are going to get when you have a third-party sorting out your gear: it could be incredible or it could end up being utter shit. When we arrived at Polideportivo Anoeta, an indoor arena in San Sebastián, for our last show on this short European leg, I realised the worst. The gear was utter shit. But while the drums were completely knackered, it was Morrissey's microphone that caused us more problems and, for Moz, a more traumatic experience. During the soundcheck, he got an electric shock from the mic. Not once, but twice. After the second major jolt, he'd had enough.

'I'm not doing this gig. It's unsafe. Let's go,' he announced.

We downed tools and left for the hotel. The idea was to get the hell out of San Sebastián as soon as possible as the cancellation was pretty late in the day. We didn't really fancy getting caught up in the aftermath once the news had broken that there wasn't going to be a show. But when we got back to the hotel, they wouldn't give us our passports. This was in the days when you had to hand them over at reception when you checked in as the ultimate deposit. It turned out that, pre-empting our flit, the venue had contacted the hotel and requested that we shouldn't be allowed to leave as we still had a show to perform. We were trapped.

In the days before social media, text messaging or email, there was no way to announce the cancellation of the gig. Fans would only find out about the development upon reaching the arena – which was exactly what happened. And they weren't happy. Things were thrown, windows were smashed, staff were verbally assaulted and unfairly held responsible. The attendant press did nothing to help calm the situation and were soon outside our hotel, riot-intent fans in tow, trying to get a glimpse of these British troublemakers who had dared insult their city. There were police at reception, but this didn't stop particularly tenacious members of the press from prowling the corridors trying to locate us. When the TV crew arrived to start filming the incident for the local news, we bolted our doors and kept our heads down.

I was relieved when the sun came up the next morning and the hotel hadn't been burnt down by 2,500 pitchfork-wielding Smiths fans. I do think the cliché that all of our fans were bedsit-bound softies clutching a slim volume of poetry to their chests at all times was one of the greatest misconceptions that surrounded the band. Some of them – many of them – were hard as fucking nails.

We never returned to Spain. In fact, we would never play – UK and Ireland aside – in Europe again.

X

A few weeks after we got back from Europe, we headed back to America for the US leg of the *Meat is Murder* tour. This was our first proper tour of the States since we'd played the Danceteria and our subsequent ill-fated, chickenpox-aborted dates. This tour began at the Aragon Ballroom in Chicago on 7 June and finished at the Universal Amphitheatre in LA on 29 June. A total of thirteen shows – Midwest to east coast to west coast, via Canada – in twenty-two days.

The gigs were a huge success. I was pleasantly shocked that the US were so familiar with our songs. Sire were in control of our catalogue and despite a modest success, the records were starting to cut through on the college circuit and more liberal, anglophile enclaves. The second night we played at New York's beautiful Beacon Theatre on the Upper West Side. We *opened* with 'Meat is Murder', having switched it from its usual place at the end of the set. Even off our home turf, I think it reflected that singular confidence that we had in what we were doing.

However, we were still viewed as slightly exotic, strange creatures by many of the people we encountered. And, of course, there was no understanding of the geography of the UK – we found a lot of Americans appeared to be under the impression that if someone lived in Britain, then they must be familiar with most people in the entire kingdom. Taking the

Beacon Theatre, featuring the Smiths and Billy Bragg, June 1985.

hotel lift down on our second morning in New York one morning, I smiled cordially at a woman as she entered.

'Hey, how's it going?' she asked me in a thick east coast drawl.

'Fine, thank you,' I replied.

As soon as she clocked my accent, she became immediately animated.

'Where are you from?' she enquired.

I hesitantly replied, 'Manchester in the UK?', as it was rare that anyone on that side of the pond knew of the existence of any other city than London.

'Oh, you're *Scottish!*' she exclaimed.

'Um...'

She pushed on. 'I know somebody called John McDonald in Edinburgh. Do you know them?'

This was how it often was.

It wasn't just our manner of speaking. We just looked different. We didn't dress how the Americans thought pop stars dressed. No shoulder pads. No Antony Price suits. No extravagantly tour-branded bomber jackets. MTV had sold them a lie. We just dressed down, as we always had, in jeans, trousers, jumpers and shoes. Yet it was somehow still apparent to the locals that, even if we couldn't possibly be pop stars, we were most certainly foreign. When we were walking down the street together, we would often be stopped and asked by strangers where we grew up. We were told repeatedly, 'You just *look* so British.' But it was not anything sartorially obvious; we had all left our monocles and top hats back in dear Old Blighty. It was more of a shared attitude, I think; a way of just being and interacting with the world. And despite the fact we all had our own individual ways in which that would manifest itself, collectively, it was one of the Smiths' great strengths. Conceptually at least, we were bigger than the sum of our parts.

A few weeks later, when we reached Los Angeles for our show at the Hollywood Palladium on Sunset Boulevard – sorry, I'll say that again, *the Hollywood Palladium on Sunset Boulevard!* – Andy and I were walking around the Melrose neighbourhood when two shy but giggly lads approached us. 'Excuse me, sir, excuse me,' one of them said as he was pushed forward by his mate. 'Are you Mike and Andy from the Smiths?'

'Yeah, yeah, sure, that's us,' I responded bashfully. We were in utter shock. I was *Hollywood* famous.

'Great, can't wait for the concert,' one of them said before walking away. As soon as I got back to the hotel, I phoned up my mam and dad just to tell them that I was in Hollywood AND that I had been recognised.

'Hollywood?!' my mother gasped. The idea that her little son from Fallowfield was on the other side of the world, cruising around this fantastical place that we had all seen only on television or in films, seemed just as unbelievable to her as it did to me. There was a feeling of achievement, an element of satisfaction. The four of us had started out to take on the world – why *couldn't* we be as big as our heroes? – and the world was starting to notice.

However, seeing how Morrissey was treated as a celebrity – even at this point – definitely made me question whether I really wanted to be any more famous. I've been to events where fans have been genuinely sweet and respectful. But in large numbers, it can become suffocating. There's a kind of devotion among Smiths fans that's rare. When people love the band, they love it deeply – and I do appreciate that. It's given me my career and, dare I say it, one day my legacy. But I've never truly felt comfortable with the lack of anonymity that sometimes I need if I'm out and about.

Mozzer couldn't go out at all. It's the burden of the frontman, of course. But particularly when the frontman is already larger than life. People tend to approach the 'character' that is presented on stage, on TV, in the press, forgetting that all *this* is part of the performance. Until you reach superstar levels of fame, you still need to go out and buy your own toilet roll. And once it starts, it's very hard to stop it. It is not in your hands to control it. But did Morrissey *want* it to stop? I don't think so. I never once heard him complain about it, even when he wasn't able to leave the house. He embraced it. He was born to be famous.

X

We learned quickly that record companies in the US operated very differently to their UK equivalent. There were so many different corporate levels to the organisation. You had to know them all, play the *game* with them all or you risked being branded difficult to work with. Rough Trade were a small, cottage industry independent in comparison to the US behemoths like Warner Bros who owned the Sire label subsidiary who we were signed to. We were used to being left to get on with the recording. We'd speak to Geoff and Scott, of course, and Martha... and Morrissey would be working with Jo on the sleeves. But in the US you were expected to meet the accountants and the lawyers and the accountants' wives and the lawyers' wives all the way up the greasy pole to the MDs and CEO. It was big business. And while we wanted the sales and the success and the fame, we wanted it on our terms. We weren't going to kiss arse just because the *suits* expected it.

Maybe it was our undoing. We just weren't malleable. We already had our own clearly defined vision as well as sound. The Americans couldn't just do whatever they wanted to with us. I don't think that they *knew* what to do with us. The combination of naïvety in how to navigate the American system and successfully play their game, coupled with the sheer *audacity* of having our own unique, entrenched identity, did not help us gain any friends on that side of the Atlantic. We were often misunderstood. Despite Seymour Stein's initial enthusiasm – I don't doubt for one minute that he loved us – he wasn't there to guide our career in a hands-on manner. Besides, the former coat-check girl who supported us at the Danceteria a few years ago was also signed to Sire and had blown up to become the biggest pop star on the planet, keeping Seymour more than busy. Naked ambition. Ultra-commercial pop songs. *Sex.* The label instinctively knew what to do with that. There was no billboard on Sunset for the Smiths. I'm just not sure Sire ever knew how to promote us.

We already had so many commitments – write–record–play, write–record–play – for the rest of 1985 that we simply could not adhere to the tried and tested American label recipe for breaking a British act. We wanted to break America, but we wanted to break it on our terms. And *nobody* breaks America on their own terms. We didn't have eighteen months free in our diary to relentlessly tour each city while making nice with the radio pluggers in Butt Fuck, Ohio. When the Police first went to crack the US, their initial run of back-to-back shows lasted two months. When they finished that first lap, they asked the label what they should do next. They were told to do the same tour all over again. In support of their 1978 debut album *Outlandos d'Amour* and the follow-up LP *Reggatta de Blanc* in 1979, the band did more than 130 gigs per year – more than

260 shows just in America to try to make a name for themselves stateside. The US is such a massive country that, by the time you have completed a substantial run of live dates, you can go back and play the same markets again as it's been nearly half a year since you were last in town. It's a well-known fact that if you want to break America, then you must woo and *work* America – and that's fair enough. We only played about thirty US gigs in total. That wasn't even foreplay. But the label never even threw enough money behind us to get to second base, let alone a shotgun wedding in Reno.

30

THE QUEEN IS DEAD

I love all the songs on our debut album, but it's my least favourite. I was never completely won over with the recording. Maybe we weren't quite ready for it, but I don't think it captured what we were capable of.

By the time we set about recording what would become *The Queen is Dead* – which initially had the working title of *Margaret on the Guillotine* – we knew what we were doing. I just felt as though we didn't have anything to prove any more.

We started work on the album in July 1985 shortly after returning from the US tour. With all the band back in Manchester, Johnny's home in Bowdon in Altrincham became a base for intense writing sessions. It was like his own one-man Brill Building. And like the practitioners of Brill, he would write with purpose and with speed. 'Frankly, Mr. Shankly', 'I Know It's Over' and 'There is a Light That Never Goes Out' were all written in one short burst at the end of the summer after the band had already committed 'The Boy With the Thorn In His Side' to tape at Drone earlier in the month. Recording was largely split between Jacobs Studio in Surrey and the legendary RAK in St John's Wood. Johnny was leading the production with Morrissey by his side and Streety was back in to engineer.

I've still got the recordings from us running through the title track in the studio and they sound fantastic. Just Johnny, Andy and myself jamming on this really heavy riff for about twenty minutes. Johnny was obsessed with his new wah-wah pedal, which on the final version he used to control the pitch of that feedback that ran all the way through the song. But the problem I had was that after playing the tom-roll for the intro, I then introduced the rest of the kit in the verse: snare rolls, tom-tom fills, cymbal crashes. But every time I played a fill, I wasn't able to continue with the running drum roll that gave the song its driving urgency. I've only got two hands; I couldn't do both! When it came time to record it, Stephen suggested that I record the intro drum toms, which he would then sample and we'd then overdub the additional parts – the cymbals and the snare. He said, 'We can get the best floor tom drum sound you've ever heard because we can isolate all the mics. It'll just be that one mic and then we can adjust the volume and the sound of it without affecting any of the rest of the kit.'

It felt a bit like cheating to me. I didn't think we should be looping anything at all. But Stephen was all about the sonics, how we could manipulate the recording technique to make it sound like the best thing you've ever heard. He also made the point that Johnny overdubbed and manipulated guitars all the time, so why shouldn't I adopt the same technique? 'Mike,' he said, 'it's just a way of getting the recording to sound great.' So that's what we did; I played the intro all the way through, Stephen sampled it and then I went in and overdubbed the cymbals, the snare, hi-hats and everything else. He was right; it sounded fucking incredible. I just tried to put out of my mind how the hell I'd play it live. When I eventually did though, I never got any complaints.

It was Morrissey's idea to do a photoshoot at the Salford Lads Club. He wanted somewhere that felt typically *northern*, a backdrop that you would have seen in Shelagh Delaney's Salford-based, late-'50s kitchen-sink drama *A Taste of Honey* – that grit and smoke and grime that characterised the post-war industrial north.

I'd never been to the Salford Lads Club before, but it could not have been a better shooting location. Unlike many neighbourhoods that were

206

knocked down and rebuilt in the 1960s, this one had preserved its original nineteenth-century architecture. It was perfect.

It was freezing and damp on the day of the shoot. Stephen Wright, who had shot us before at the Free Trade Hall the previous year, was the photographer. Morrissey had decided we'd take a picture directly outside the club, its name prominent in the shot. It was only afterwards that I noticed it was actually on the corner of Coronation Street – not the fictional television street itself but a cool coincidence nonetheless.

While we were there, a couple of local lads turned up on bikes and watched us closely. This was their patch and we weren't from around there. In those days, if you showed up somewhere unfamiliar, people wanted to know why. It seemed like nothing had changed – no matter how old you got – since my own Salford run-in round there when I was a teenager.

The shoot itself was simple. This was pre-digital so Stephen likely shot only a couple of rolls of film – maybe twenty-four photos per roll. Half an hour and done. There wasn't any elaborate styling or planning. We certainly didn't discuss what we were each going to wear beforehand. I was wearing a jacket that cost 70p from a charity shop. Nothing was curated or planned.

It became perhaps the defining image of the Smiths and, after forty years, I also think it's one of *the* all-time great band photos. A photo on its own isn't iconic. It only becomes iconic through its wider context. If that picture had been used for a terrible record, I doubt we'd still be talking about it. And bear in mind that we were still seven months away from releasing the album. We'd only released 'The Boy With the Thorn in His Side' as an early teaser single. But I look at that picture of us on that shitty cold day and see a band on the cusp of their absolute prime.

31

CRAIG

1986

It was around the time of recording *The Queen is Dead* that the issue with Andy and heroin had come to a head. I do find it slightly uncomfortable talking about such a personal situation, especially since he's not around anymore, but pretty much everything has been openly discussed about this period before.

By looking at him, you would never guess that Andy struggled with addiction. He looked so healthy, so youthful and so *not* what you would expect someone battling a heroin problem to look like. Government health warning posters around this time always depicted the typical addict sweating, covered in spots, greasy hair and with dirty clothes. This wasn't Andy at all. He hid it so well. He always only took just enough, it seemed, to remain on a semi-even keel.

His saving grace was that he was never what I would call *greedy* with the drug. I've seen people start using recreationally, but then it escalates. Just a *little* bit more. For some reason, Andy didn't have to do that. I remember us driving back from gigs and each of us getting dropped off at our respective homes. It always seemed obvious what he was going to do when he arrived home. He would start getting a bit restless in the van. I'd start to think, *Chill out*. But we never addressed what was going on, even though we knew exactly what was happening.

Initially, Andy's addiction didn't have a huge impact on his personality or affect his musicianship. However, when it did, I felt like it had become my business. I had tried to address the problem with him around 1986. One night, I went round to his place to have it out with him. At this time, Andy lived in a basement flat with no windows. In the bay outlook, where the windows *should've* been, there was a brick wall covered by closed full-length curtains. I didn't like the atmosphere in there one bit. It was grim. There were strung-out folk littered about the place who clearly had no interest in his musical pursuits. I took him to one side and said, 'This can't go on, mate. If you don't jack this in and get rid of this lot, then I really don't think I can be your friend anymore.'

It was clear from his reaction and the look on his face that he didn't really give a shit whether I was his friend or not.

What had once seemed under control had, inevitably, taken over and redefined Andy. I realised that this was no longer my mate. In retrospect, it was naïve of us to think things weren't going to reach this level of escalation. Any communication between us was now between the addict and me, not Andy and me. Addiction is like being at the bottom of a 20-foot well. Your friends can encourage you up all they like, reassure you everything will be fine. You'll probably believe them. You might even want to join them. But they're not coming down into the well and you haven't got a ladder to get out. It's a long, hard climb. It's very easy to get angry and frustrated when somebody who you love and admire just can't seem to do the right thing to rid themselves of the thing that is causing everyone around them such tremendous heartache. But, as I've said, we were no longer dealing with the Andy that we knew and loved. He was prepared to throw everything away to carry on using.

To Andy's credit, he worked hard to come off the heroin, but it was soon substituted with methadone. This unfortunately only made matters worse. His playing especially suffered. In early 1986, we headed over to Ireland for a couple of gigs. Before the Dublin show, it became noticeable during the soundcheck that Andy's playing was badly affected. He was slurring his words and missing notes. It sounded – and looked – terrible.

The rest of us discussed the situation and agreed to relieve Andy of his position. It was decided that enough was enough. Smiths legend has always framed Morrissey as delivering the news in a rather cowardly manner via a postcard left on his car windshield: 'Andy you have left the Smiths. Goodbye and good luck, Morrissey.' In 2004, Andy confirmed this *did* happen, so I'm happy to let him have the final word on the matter.

Andy was devastated, but I really felt we were left with no choice. We all did. I think we hoped that by forcing his hand in this manner the gravity of the situation would make him clean up his act. Adding insult to injury, a few days after he was fired, he found himself present at a house that was raided by the police. Everyone was arrested. Everyone – including Andy – thought that he'd end up doing time for it. Luckily, he got a two-year suspended sentence and a £1,000 fine. It was a massive relief and the almighty scare and huge kick up the arse that he needed to straighten himself out.

The worry now though was that even if Andy got his act together in time, he might be refused a visa to enter the US for the upcoming summer *Queen is Dead* tour.

Alternative options were discussed and Guy Pratt's name came up. Guy would go on to work with Pink Floyd, but Johnny knew him via a session they had both done with Bryan Ferry. Guy was a really accomplished player and, for almost two weeks, he rehearsed with us, attempting to learn all of Andy's intricate parts. Andy was even generously on hand to teach him. But there was one huge glaring issue: he had a ponytail. This made for a barrier that was impossible to overcome. It was, 'No way. That's not happening.'

However, with Craig Gannon, it was the opposite. He looked great.

Craig was brought in by Johnny to assist on guitar. Not only would his introduction fatten the sound of the Smiths musically, but it also gave Johnny freedom when playing live, allowing him to more faithfully replicate the songs as they were on record.

My first impression of Craig was that he was incredibly cool – like he belonged in the Smiths without even trying. And none of it felt forced. He was younger than us, by just a couple of years, but when you're in your early twenties, that still feels significant. I first heard of him when he was touring America with Aztec Camera and supporting Elvis Costello – he was just sixteen at the time.

Craig was from Salford. Like the rest of us, he was very northern and a brilliant guitarist. On the live *Rank* album, which was released in 1988, his playing was flawless. Technically, he was probably the closest I'd seen to Johnny in terms of dexterity. There wasn't anything outside his ability. He also had great gear – lovely semi-hollow guitars and the like.

Personally, I got on really well with him. He had a very dry sense of humour – quiet, a bit unusual, but sharp. Even post-Smiths, we remained in touch and worked together in the studio, not least of all on Mozzer's early solo material.

Johnny once mentioned in interviews that it didn't work out with Craig because they wanted him to be more assertive. But that's not who Craig is – he's naturally shy. It certainly wasn't about skill. He's a phenomenal musician. I remember once he pointed out the ending theme tune of *Bullseye*, the old darts game show. He said that when the contestants win, they play the theme in a major key and if they lose, it is in a minor key. That was such a typically Craig thing to notice. I also saw him once sit down and play the theme tune to the children's cartoon *Captain Pugwash* perfectly from memory. The song was a complicated sea shanty, but he nailed it. He could walk into any room, hear something once and just play it. He had a next-level talent.

When it seemed like Andy was serious about resolving his own personal issues, he was welcomed back into the fold. He was only out for a few weeks. I'm going to say that the police raid was one the best things that could have happened to him. At the same time, Andy's US visa application was accepted and we were free to tour the States again.

32

AMERICAN DREAMING

Queen is Dead US tour, 1986.
© Nalinee Darmrong

Ongoing disputes with Rough Trade meant we had to delay the release of *The Queen is Dead* before it finally came out in June, entering the UK chart at number two. We were held off the top spot by Genesis but, in a nice piece of symbolism, we did manage to knock Queen down to number three, which seemed only right.

After a few dates in the UK, including a tenth anniversary celebration of punk with New Order at Manchester's G-Mex and a storming gig at Salford Uni the next night, we took *The Queen is Dead* tour overseas to Canada and the US in the summer of 1986. We had twenty-six dates lined up in total. We hadn't quite given up on America yet. When we played off the back of *Meat is Murder* in 1985, the title alone piqued the interest of a more 'alternative' US audience. As a follow-up, *The Queen is Dead* – equally provocatively titled – had garnered even more attention across the Atlantic. On pretty much every college radio chart we'd be sparring with R.E.M. for the top two spots. Our respective tours would even carefully dance around each other come September. R.E.M. were supporting their fourth album *Lifes Rich Pageant* – a very successful 'alternative' band at that point, but a few years away from *Out of Time* and their crossover superstardom. But they were still receiving a healthy amount of support from their own record label IRS. It felt very much at odds with the support we were receiving from Sire and, given R.E.M. were as equally as idiosyncratic as we were, we continued to wonder what we were doing wrong. In retrospect, it was fairly clear what it was that we were doing wrong...

A trifecta of unfortunate incidents, all occurring in one single evening, indelibly marked us as English arseholes in the eyes of many people who worked at our US label Sire. First up, we were expected to partake in a 'meet and greet' for around thirty people from the label before our show. This gathering could consist of anyone from the CEO to some random guy from the marketing department and the random guy's wife. 'We just want to say "Hi!"' is what the label rep told us about this potpourri of strangers planning to storm our dressing room. However, there was a problem: we didn't *want* to say 'Hi!'. We weren't exactly 'saying Hi!' sort of guys at the best of times, especially when we were basically getting ready to play a gig. We didn't want to see anybody, particularly a bunch of randoms we did not know and would be unlikely to ever see again. We were preparing for the show and didn't want any distractions, which we quite emphatically, and possibly quite tactlessly, made clear. This bucking of corporate label tradition was seen as incredibly rude. Strike one.

Backstage, a well-meaning label representative had left a stack of pictures, with the request that we sign them. When we picked the first one up to start the task, we noticed that what had been presented to us was an image from more than two years ago and not the new shots that we had taken to promote the album and current tour. Fuck's sake! 'Why do they not have the most recent ones?' Nope, bollocks to that, we decided. The old 8×10s were chucked unceremoniously into the bin. Strike two.

The dressing room we were set up in was adorned with modernist furniture, fixtures and fittings, giving it a somewhat sleek if cold, minimal ambience. Adding to this vibe was a glass table, which Craig casually attempted to sit on before the gig. I say 'attempt', because as his backside made contact with the smooth surface, the entire piece shattered under his weight, sending him crashing to the floor in a cascade of splintered shards. Obviously, he did not destroy it on purpose, but as we were just about to go on stage, he picked himself up, carefully dusted himself down and walked out to the stage. Unintentional strike three.

So, in one evening, we had left in our wake a bunch of pissed-off label executives – and wives – several dozen band glossies in the bin and a dressing room that, for all intents and purposes, would be reported as having been 'trashed'.

This very quickly led to rampant rumours about how ghastly we were to work with. We didn't do ourselves any favours, but we were also just not going to say '*Yes*' to every request while tugging our forelocks. That's not what we do in Manchester. But equally, we weren't *trying* to be rude. However, 'What do you mean the limey bastards don't want to see us? Don't they know who we are?' 'They tore the photos up and tossed them in the bin? Didn't even sign them?' 'THEY SMASHED UP THE FUCKING DRESSING ROOM?!' It doesn't sound so great, does it? If it had been me, I'd be thinking *fuck those guys*, too.

The label did not know where we fitted on their marketing matrix – we were destructive idiots who would not even do the most basic things to help with promoting our own record.

Conversely, I think a lot of Americans liked us because we were English and, well, a bit peculiarly individual, the same way that we were intrigued by US artists like the New York Dolls, the Ramones, Blondie, Iggy Pop and the Velvets.

Initially, I found it quite hard to comprehend our appeal in America. How can you be a Smiths fan if you're American? I know that sounds like a ridiculous statement, but back then I found it difficult for US fans to make the connection since we were so far removed from each other in our cultural upbringing. American Smiths fans simply couldn't understand what being from Manchester was like. How do they understand songs like 'The Headmaster Ritual', which is all about corporal punishment? Was that even a thing in the US the way it was in the UK? 'Rusholme Ruffians?' Rusholme is a suburb next to Fallowfield. When we were growing up, there was a park called Platt Fields which would host a funfair once a year. I used to attend it when I was a kid. It would be filled with knife-wielding rival gangs; the aggression and bloodshed a sharp contrast to the jovial atmosphere. Morrissey loved the clash and contradiction between the two extremes. The wonderment and faded incandescent beauty of the fairground at night alongside the violence and intimidation of the marauding gang of toughs. That is how that song got its name. I don't think you could get a more English-sounding word than 'ruffian'. Then match it up with a place nobody had heard of; it was incredibly parochial.

But as I got older, I started to recognise the similarities. How was listening to 1960s Motown when I was marooned in my bedroom in Manchester really any different? These bands and acts wrote hits that transcended geography. Same with early rock 'n' roll, some of Moz and Johnny's biggest influences. We didn't understand any of the things these US acts were singing about from our own experience, but we picked up on the feel of the language. Whether it was abstract or more direct – 'you go to a club on your own, and you leave on your own, you go home, and you want to die' from 'How Soon is Now?' is no different from 'I'll be so lonely, I could die' from 'Heartbreak Hotel' – you realise that all great songs include that universality.

X

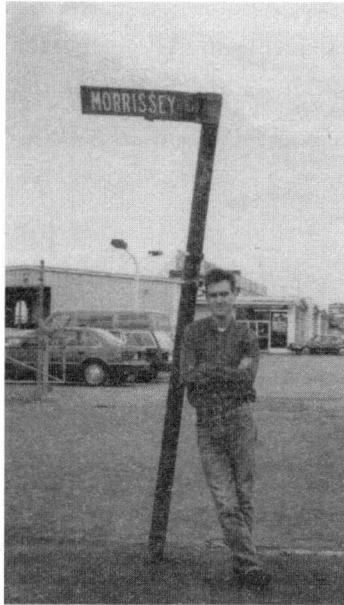

Morrissey Boulevard, Boston, 1985.

On 5 August, we were booked into Mansfield, near Boston, at the Great Woods Performing Arts Center. Although we'd played three Canadian gigs at the start of the tour, this was the first date of the US leg. This was a magnificent outdoor venue that held about 12,000 people and we had sold it out. It was by far the biggest US date we'd undertaken. We were doing *something* right.

It was a beautiful balmy evening when we took to the stage. I normally got some pre-show nerves, but somehow, looking out at this incredible spectacle – everything I had always dreamed of – it only galvanised me. I felt more determined and focused than nervous.

The Smiths never had any pre-performance rituals as such, no gathering around in a circle thanking God and whooping, so our walk-on music was important. In the early days, it was Cilla Black's 'Love of the Loved', but since the year before we'd been making our entrance to Prokofiev. We kept with this for the rest of our career – you can hear it open our live album *Rank* – but here, in this atmosphere, a *sea* of American fans in front of us, its rousing grandiosity set the hairs up on my arms. Even now when I hear that music, I still start to get a bit emotional.

Just prior to going on, we heard that some kids had been found to be incapacitated due to taking PCP, or Angel Dust as it was also called. PCP was one of those drugs that you'd hear about and think, *I'm not sure* that *sounds like much fun*. It was also an almost exclusively American drug so our exposure to it in the UK had been limited. Even though I had never shied away from the odd dabble with other stimulants, this drug, with its notorious effects of unhinged super-human strength, convulsions and – *what fun!* – losing bodily control, did not appeal to me one bit. And it was on the loose at our show.

By 1986, we had developed a fearsome reputation as a live act. Not just as players but for the spectacle we created, the tinderbox we would ignite each night on stage, the crowd so whipped up into a frenzy by Moz's own dedicated performance – part singer, part ringmaster – that more and more kids wanted to get as close as possible to the stage and the band and, ultimately, get on the stage itself. It's almost impossible to describe just how emotionally charged the atmosphere was at a Smiths gig. The sheer fucking *passion*. The stage invasions came about due to a complete abandonment of the usual social constraints experienced by the audiences at our gigs. And I had the best seat in the house to view this spectacle. When fans made it on stage, Johnny would sometimes groove along with their dance moves. Or, more often than not, they would make a beeline for Mozzer and drape themselves around his neck, clinging on for dear life, wanting that short precious moment of contact with *him* to last for ever. I didn't recall seeing that kind of behaviour from fans of any of the other countless bands that I'd seen live. It was an almost religious fervour, a pent-up release of ecstasy from the congregation that would engulf the altar. We completely embraced the spectacle.

As we were nearing the end of the set in Mansfield, a small gaggle of revellers joined us on the stage. This was nothing unusual. But then one of the guys ran at me on the drum riser. He was grimacing, clenching his fists and gritting his teeth. Less ecstatic mania more outright maniacal.

He jumped up on top of my stage monitor, a speaker cabinet standing at about five feet.

You might think *that's* impressive in its own right – but he wasn't on the drum riser to start with. If you add the height of that, he'd jumped straight up with no running start to a height of about seven feet. He was inches from me, close enough to give me a kiss if the mood had struck him. Initially, I just thought he was having the time of his life and getting right into the music. And, you know, some of those American lads *were* quite athletic, but when I saw the expression on his face, I got slightly concerned for my own safety. His whole face was twisted and distorted and gurning like crazy. I wasn't exactly sure what his next move was going to be.

At one of our US gigs in 1986 with sound engineer Tim Whitten. Look at the height of my drum monitor, add in the extra two feet for the riser I am sitting on and you can get an idea of how high the guy on PCP had jumped.

This sort of close encounter during a show didn't normally happen to me because I was sat at the back of the stage. It's usually something that the lads at the front had to deal with. I couldn't stop playing because I was in the middle of a song, but fortunately security noticed him before he was able to... what? Rip my drums apart? Rip *me* apart? I guess in that PCP-fuelled moment he didn't know either. It took four guys to get him off.

That was one wild show.

It's moments like these that are incredibly difficult to describe to anyone who hasn't been there themselves. All the years of working with bands that never quite made it, standing outside in the rain at the rehearsal rooms, the disappointments, the frustrations, the boredom of travelling hundreds of hours in a van up and down the country, eating crap food, the hanging around in studios, the fretting about not getting the right take, the hanging around at soundchecks... I mean, I could go on. And on. But all the shit things you've had to endure to get to this point are completely forgotten in these moments. Every musician I have ever spoken to says the same thing. It's a moment you wish you could bottle and keep for ever.

We hit New York the next day and travelled to the soundcheck.

The Smiths were *nowhere* near the top of the main Billboard album charts – *The Queen is Dead* peaked at number seventy – yet the show we were due to play was an outdoor gig on the Hudson River at a place called Pier 84 with an 8,000 capacity. Running alongside the venue was a docked and decommissioned Second World War aircraft carrier.

The whole place was awe-inspiring. I had to pinch myself that we were playing an open-air, sold-out show on the banks of the Hudson River in New York City. The view from every angle was jaw-dropping, with the water stretching out towards the west. We'd played outdoor gigs before, but nowhere as visually stunning as this; the towers of mid-town Manhattan behind us, Blondie's Union City and New Jersey over the river from us. I had always had a massive belief in the band, but to be faced with such a beautiful physical manifestation of that hope can be quite overwhelming.

I went on a hunt to see if any members of the NY road crew had any pot. They very kindly made a spliff and handed it to me. It was what we call in the UK 'a one skinner': just a single cigarette paper filled with weed.

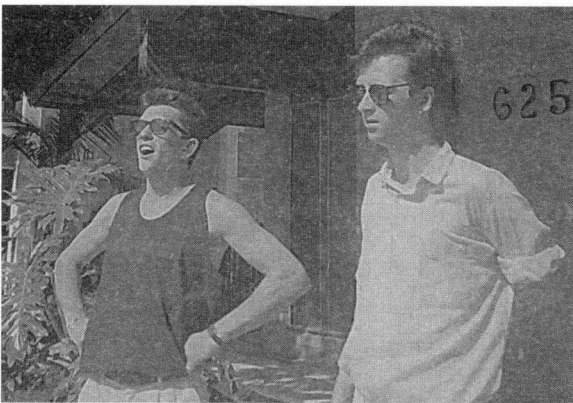

Me and Johnny, US tour, 1986.

I was reminded of Jim Morrison's quote: 'You can pick your teeth with a New York joint.' On this occasion, I did not use it for cleaning my gnashers, but my God, it was strong. I was used to mixing tobacco with weed and making a fat one. I think that's a very 'British' thing to do. But this was unadulterated and strong as hell. I knew I wouldn't be smoking anymore of that before the gig, but it sure did enhance my already blissed-out state as I gazed across the Hudson.

I went back to the hotel and started watching the TV when a woman appeared on the screen asking the question, 'What is this phenomenon called the Smiths?' *Woah, That's me!* I thought.

She went on to explain that this band had sold out New York's infamous Pier 84 without even having a record in the charts. She mentioned that it was tonight's hot ticket in town if you were one of the lucky ones to have secured entrance for the sold-out show. It was quite funny, but totally surreal. Lying on my hotel bed, stoned, watching a reporter on American TV bestowing such an accolade on the band that I was the drummer for. I thought about calling my parents again – just to remind them that I'd *arrived* on the east coast as well as the west – but thought better of it, the after-effects of my formidable one-skinner still cheerfully fugging my brain.

When we arrived at the gig, we heard that there were quite a few celebrities that had muscled their way onto the guestlist. Mick Jagger – *Mick Jagger!* – was one of them. The record company handler stuck his head around the dressing room door and asked us if he could come and say hello before the gig. *This time* we made an exception. 'Yeah, sure,' all four of us tried to casually answer, though we were of course all dying inside. The rock god came into the dressing room and we were all trying to be nonchalant about it. You know, 'Oh, this just happens to us all the time. No big deal!'

'Hi Mick, nice to meet you,' I said.

Mick Jagger!

He was dressed smart but casual, the sort of smart/casual that probably cost more to attain than our entire tour earnings. His face was wrinkled in what seemed like a permanent, frozen state of happiness.

As you can imagine, Jagger possessed an air of cool that could only be carried off by knowing you are one of the most famous musicians that has ever lived – and not only that but someone who wrote the guidebook for what we were doing. We in turn were just trying our hardest not to look completely fazed by his presence. It was just too surreal. He naturally honed in on Morrissey and they had a brief chat. As he left the dressing room, he told us to 'have a good one', like one old trouper passing on his patronage to the new kids. 'Cheers, Mick!' I said as if we were old showbiz pals who would be meeting up in the bar afterwards for a long night of carousing.

Everything was perfect. The sound was great, the weather was idyllic, the crowd were going ape. I still could not quite believe we were able to command such love and hysteria so far from home.

When we played 'Still Ill', Johnny came over to me and flicked his head, gesturing for me to look at the side of the stage. And who do I see grooving away? Well, it's my old mate Jagger. He was not just grooving, though, he was doing a Mick Jagger dance. I watched for a while and started to think, *I'm making Mick Jagger dance*. Equally, it crossed my mind that if I *stopped* playing at any moment, then Mick was going to stop dancing. *I* had this power over him. *Dance, Jagger, dance*, I thought.

We played the Aragon Ballroom in Chicago about halfway through the tour. This place was a lovely old music theatre, still retaining all of its original 1920s charm. I always enjoy playing in the faded grandeur of the old-style theatres: baroque architecture, soaring ceilings, velvet curtains, a hushed, faded elegance, places just buzzing with ambient history. Legend had it that a tunnel ran beneath the venue to nearby Green Mill bar, a Prohibition-era hangout of none other than Al Capone who could often be seen in the venue's VIP box before nipping off for

Aragon Ballroom ticket stub.

an undercover hooch. It turned out to be one of the hottest, rowdiest shows of the tour. Not only did we have to keep dodging a steady rain of airborne beer – Capone would not have approved – but a huge pile of temporary seating was destroyed at the back of the hall after everyone had left. The desolation inside was eerily reflected on the down-at-heel neighbourhood that surrounded the venue. The streets were ominously deserted, except for a few homeless people passed out on the sidewalk and in dime store doorways.

We should have noticed the signs weren't great after we had finished our soundcheck earlier in the afternoon. Morrissey headed off back to the hotel on the tour bus, while me, Andy and Johnny hung out at the venue, soaking in the atmosphere. After a while, alongside our tour manager Stuart, we all decided to follow our lead singer back to where we were staying and chill out for a bit before the show. We asked a guy who worked at the venue if he could get us a cab.

'Sorry, fellas, no can do,' he told us. 'Taxis won't stop for me.'

He didn't need to explain why. He was about 6 foot 6 and of Native American heritage. Even though *we* were foreigners in this land and didn't completely understand the racial complexities over there, we understood what he was implying. And the irony that it would have been fine for a bunch of lads from England to get a cab and not someone whose people were indigenous to America was not lost on us.

226

We told him that we had to get back to the hotel to have something to eat, a shower and a change of clothes.

'You might be able to get a cab if *you* all go out front and try to flag one down. But don't go past the traffic lights at the intersection whatever you do. Seriously, *don't* go past the intersection,' he warned.

So we were hanging around on the sidewalk and there was no sign of a cab whatsoever. We were looking longingly towards that intersection that we had been advised to avoid unless we wanted to die, but it looked like there was a lot more going on up there and it certainly seemed to offer the best option of getting this elusive cab.

We were all staring towards the oasis of this crossroads, licking our lips and just waiting for one of us to say, 'Fuck it, come on, let's head over' when about half a dozen guys emerged from the forbidden zone, crossed the road and started walking towards us.

'Hey, whatsup?' one of them asked.

'Erm, nothing at the moment,' we replied.

I noted from the change in the expression on their faces that they didn't bump into Mancunians that often around there.

'Where the *hell* you from?'

'We're from Manchester.'

'Oh, you're from Connecticut?!'

'No, we're from the UK.'

'From *where?*'

One guy asked me if I wanted a doobie. I was struck dumb with mild fear and incomprehension. *What the fuck is a doobie? And would it hurt? Fuck, the guy in the venue was right.*

Johnny nudged me and whispered, 'It's a spliff.'

'Oh, nah, I'm okay, thanks man,' I jovially replied, trying to hide my building apprehension.

Right on cue, a cab arrived to relieve us from any further impending nonsense and we made our way to the hotel.

Stuart later told us that he was glad our little interaction with these dudes was so amiable before the cab turned up as he had been carrying the upfront gig payment of $25,000 in cash in the bag that he had been holding the entire time. I'm not sure our easy British charm could have talked us out of that one if they'd asked what was in Stuart's bag.

We used to have goodie bags waiting for us backstage after a show because we often didn't eat just prior to going on. The routine of playing gigs has never been conducive to maintaining proper, regulated mealtimes. Who is going to eat a big meal at 8 p.m. when you're going on at 9 p.m.? The last thing you want is to feel bloated on stage. For me, being sat down for ninety minutes would be a challenge; I can't imagine what it would have been like for Moz. The problem was of course that the kitchens of most of the places we would stay at would usually be closed by the time we got back after the gig, leaving us often manically hungry. At some point, one of us came up with the simple idea of having an array of personalised snacks (and sometimes other sundries) ready for us to grab backstage as we left a venue – we called them our 'goody bags'. This was pretty much the most demanding stipulation on our rider. Tales of outlandish rock 'n' roll riders are legion but, for us, there was joy in comfort and simplicity and the knowledge that we wouldn't be fucking starving until breakfast after finishing up a gig and heading back to the hotel. And for as long as I toured with the Smiths, *nothing* tasted sweeter on the road than something from that bag post-gig. They didn't contain anything fancy: a cheese sandwich, a packet of cigarettes, a can of Coke, a couple of beers, chocolate, crisps and some fruit. That was mine. Johnny had a strict 'no mayonnaise' policy for his sandwiches and so did Morrissey. It was always difficult to wind down after a show and the goodie bag ended up becoming an important part of the post-gig ritual for all of us.

We did a couple of shows at the Universal Amphitheatre in Los Angeles in late August. Everything about LA was next-level: the weather, the hotel, the crowds, the recognition. Being there was a shock, but in a good way. Everything looked so different – clean, tidy, almost utopian. We didn't see the rough areas, so it felt like sunshine, swimming pools and cool buildings everywhere. We stayed at the Le Parc Hotel in West Hollywood, close to Rodeo Drive. It had a rooftop jacuzzi and a beautiful pool. It felt like a dream.

Even the little things stood out. Shopping was incredible. In the UK, trying to buy Levi's was a nightmare – you'd get a 38-inch waist with a 26-inch leg, which fits no one. But in America, they had odd-number sizing – 28, 29, 31 – sizes that actually made sense. The selection was amazing and everything was cheaper. You could get a pair of Levi's for £15–£20, compared to three times that in the UK. Same with Ray-Bans – huge variety and dirt cheap.

What really stood out was the service. The US is a service-based

Taking a call at Le Parc Hotel.

economy and there was nowhere you would notice that more than in LA. In the UK, two shops five doors apart can offer the same wares and offer the same experience and survive. In the US, only the very best one survives – because people care about service and quality. The customer is everything. Have a nice day!

In restaurants, they'd ask, 'Would you like to hear the specials?' and rattle off a full list from memory. In the UK, they might point to a board or say, 'It's over there.' In Los Angeles, they'd learned it, because it mattered. Everyone was prepared. They wanted your business and it felt like they *genuinely* cared whether you had a good experience.

Of course, coming from the UK where we treated strangers with suspicion, customers as a nuisance and diners as an inconvenience, we had never, *ever*, experienced anything like it. It was fucking surreal in the best possible way.

After a successful gig in New Orleans, we hit the town as we had a day off the following day before our gig in St Petersburg in Florida. The promoter asked me if I've ever heard of a drink called a 'Hurricane'. I couldn't say I had, but, given where we were, it would have been rude not to try one, wouldn't it? Local speciality and all that. He ordered a round for me and Andy. It was like a Long Island iced tea but made with about eight spirits and with blackcurrant juice on the top.

Andy and I were drinking one Hurricane after another forgetting the crucial difference between how spirits were decanted in the UK versus in the US. In the UK, everything is carefully dribbled into a universal measure. In the US, free pouring was *de rigueur* with no advised barrier to generous servings. No wonder these were called Hurricanes; I could feel the liberal servings already giving me a wallop.

The bar that we were in was absolutely rammed. I told Andy I was going outside to take some air for five minutes.

When I got out to the pavement, the streets were buzzing with New Orleans nightlife. I noticed two huge policemen standing over an obviously drunk girl who was sitting basically passed out on the ground, slumped against the wall. Then, for whatever reason, one of the cops gave this girl an almighty kick.

I tried to reason with this cop: 'Fucking hell, come on man, she's not doing you any harm!' The cop told me to mind my own business.

'But she's not exactly a threat to you, is she?' I retorted.

The next thing I knew, he grabbed me and threw me over the boot of his NOPD vehicle. He kicked my legs open, spread-eagle fashion, pulled both my arms behind my back, slapped on the cuffs and bundled me into the patrol car. Well, that escalated quickly.

After a few minutes, another guy in cuffs was thrown in the back, shortly followed by the formerly comatose girl. The cops got in the car and off we went.

I was completely freaked out. Where were they taking us? Nobody at the bar knew where I was. When I failed to return, what would they do? There was no way of contacting me. I had just disappeared.

The cop on the passenger side turned around to look at me through the metal grill.

'Where are you from?' he asked.

'I'm from Manchester, England. My band has just played a gig in town.'

'Oh yeah?' he smirked. 'What band?'

'We are called the Smiths,' I said.

Not a flicker.

The very drunk girl, who had said nothing so far, suddenly woke up and screamed, 'He's fuckin' lying! I was at that concert and he's NOT in the band!'

She then tried to headbutt me. I couldn't defend myself in any way as I was handcuffed.

The cop was shouting at her to pipe down, which thankfully she did before promptly falling back into a state of unconsciousness. *Well, so much for trying to be a knight in shining armour*, I thought.

The car started to slow down. We were pulling in somewhere. I noticed a very large neon sign: 'Bail Bonds Available Here'.

Oh God. I'm going to jail.

I was taken inside, my cuffs were removed and I was put into what I recognised from American films as the holding tank. It was about 20 by 15 feet, with maybe ten other guys of varying states of presentability and intoxication slouched on benches within.

Being very familiar with this situation, albeit from a fictional perspective, I knew nonetheless exactly what I needed to do. Avoid grief from fellow inmates by presenting as the meanest motherfucker in the slammer. *If you know what is good for you, you'll stay the motherfucking way out of my motherfucking face!* So, um yeah, that's what I did.

One of my cellmates came up to me and asked for a smoke. I casually threw a cigarette at him in a slightly surly fashion. *TAKE THAT!*

There was a payphone on the wall and I had a few quarters in my pocket. I had no idea who I was going to call. I didn't have anyone's phone numbers and I couldn't remember the name of the hotel. I didn't even know the name of the bar we'd just been in.

Okay! On the telly, what does a Brit abroad do when he finds himself in a sticky situation? He calls the British Embassy.

'Hello, operator? Could you put me through to the British Embassy, please?'

'I'm sorry, what was that sir, the British Embassy?'

'Yes, please.'

'I'll certainly try, sir.'

'Could you hold for me one moment please, sir?'

'Errr, not really.'

'One moment, sir.'

I waited. And waited. And waited. And then the line went dead. Shit. I rather feared my over-compensatingly polite telephone manner had scuppered my Most Ruthless Hood in New Orleans vibe as well.

I sat down back on the bench and wondered what Andy and the promoter were thinking. How long would it take – after a skinful of Hurricanes – to have the wherewithal to call the local police station and enquire whether or not a skinny, pasty-faced drummer had been mistakenly incarcerated that evening?

After what felt like a lifetime, a cop opened the holding-cell door and pointed me in the direction of what I presumed was the charge desk. Another cop behind the table asked me my name. I managed that. My address in New Orleans? No idea, I'm afraid. The cop then asked me if I was a fag.

Nope.

'Well, you *look* like a fag.'

'You're wrong,' I assured him.

'Am I? You callin' me a liar, then?'

Alarm bells were ringing.

'No, of course not, officer. You're just mistaken.'

I was charged with being drunk in a public place and interfering with a police investigation. I told the cop that I had a concert to play the day after tomorrow and I was leaving in the morning, so I really needed to get out of there ASAP.

'Is that so?!' he barked with glee.

Bail was set for what I later learned to be an unusually high amount for such a misdemeanour. And then it was back to the holding cell. Clearly an arbitrary 'Pop Star Bail' had been set for me.

Later on that night – or earlier/later the next morning? – the cell door opened.

'Mike Joyce?'

'Yep?'

'Out you come. You've been bailed.'

It was the best news I think I'd ever heard in my life! Stuart James, our besieged tour manager, was there with someone from the venue looking at me with a 'What the fuck have you been doing, you dick?' kind of face.

Apparently, Andy had come outside to see where the hell I was and luckily for me he was just in time to see the cop car pulling away with the back of my head visible in the rear window.

All in all, I had been the worst fake hardest felon in the Deep South.

After New Orleans, we went on to play what would be our final date of the tour in St Petersburg. We were in fact due to play a further run of four shows in Miami, Atlanta, Nashville and New York, but these shows were eventually cancelled. There were a number of explanations that were officially and unofficially offered – including an excuse that Andy had been stung by a stingray – but ultimately the relentlessness of our schedule had pushed us to the edge and we needed a proper break.

However, Andy *did* indeed get stung by a stingray. The day after our St Petersburg gig, we both went down to the beach on Tampa Bay to have a look around. When we got down there, the water looked so inviting that we decided to take a dip. It was lovely and warm and a perfect respite from the humid Florida fug. As we were walking back up the beach out of the water, Andy suddenly let out this blood-curdling scream. He managed to hobble out of the water and I rushed over to him to see blood streaming out of the sole of his foot. It looked to me like he'd stood on a shard of glass. We sat down on the beach and he was obviously in absolute agony as he was shaking like a leaf. Some locals came running over and had a look at his foot and told us he had probably been stung by one of the local stingrays. The emergency services were promptly called. As we were sitting on the beach, Andy started to panic and explained that the pain was advancing from his foot up to his knee. Then, all of a sudden, it was up in his thigh and heading into his groin as the venom started making its way into his bloodstream. The paramedics arrived shortly after and whisked Andy away. He was discharged later that day and caught up with us at the hotel. The doctors had told him that he had had a lucky escape as although the barb had penetrated his foot quite deeply, it hadn't broken off inside, which would have been much worse and would have required surgery to get all the fragments removed.

Stingrays and arrests aside, the American tour was a massive success. Bill Graham, the world-renowned concert promoter, worked with us at one of the gigs and said off-handedly, 'The next time you play over here, it'll be stadiums.' It was just a matter-of-fact throwaway statement from the irascible industry legend who had only promoted the likes of, oh you know, Bob Dylan, Neil Young, the Who, Led Zeppelin and countless other titans of rock. But what we *could* achieve in the US was really starting to hit home. If we could sell out 12,000-seater venues on both coasts without any serious financial clout from a record company and virtually no mainstream airplay, imagine what we could do if we *had* a half-decent level of support? We were in awe of America for many reasons. I think we all went home elated at the possibilities of what the future held.

X

We returned to Britain and did a series of shows throughout October to wrap up *The Queen is Dead* tour. We did three nights at three different venues in London, the last of which was at the London Palladium. Like our appearance at the Royal Albert Hall the previous year, the Palladium was an unusual venue for a rock band to play, especially for one with our alternative status. Tucked in between Oxford Street and Carnaby Street in central London, I'm pretty sure it was Morrissey's choice to do a gig there. It wasn't a *huge* venue, but what it lacked in capacity it made up for in its rich history. There used to be a show called *Sunday Night at the London Palladium*, which was broadcast from the theatre and watched by about a third of the entire nation. *The Royal Variety Performance* was held there between 1928 and 2019. All the light entertainment greats have graced its boards – from Arthur Askey to Norman Wisdom, Tommy Steele to Liberace.

Of course it was Morrissey's idea.

33

STRANGEWAYS,
HERE WE COME

It has been widely acknowledged that all four band members regard *Strangeways, Here We Come* as our finest album. I sometimes jokingly refer to this assessment as the only thing we all definitely agree on. The time spent in the studio working on the record were probably the most enjoyable sessions I'd experienced with the band. This is ironic given how close it came to the end. But by this point, our communication musically was almost telepathic.

Sessions started in spring 1987 in the village of Beckington in Somerset at the Wool Hall Studios, named for its origins as an eighteenth-century location for trading sheep fleece. It was a great atmosphere in the studio, which had this unbelievable in-house catering team. Because of this, it was almost impossible to get any work done after dinner. We did try a couple of times, but we were basically left comatose after the slap-up meals that were put on for us. Most days we'd start playing after breakfast and then have a light lunch. Our most creative and productive windows were our afternoon sessions after lunch. If Mozzer had an early night, in the evening we did a lot of jamming in the live room while sinking a few beers. There were no big parties as we were there to work and it would've meant the next day being a write-off. So most evenings we would just be laying down more overdubs, playing covers for the fun of it and generally enjoying ourselves after Morrissey had retired post-dinner.

It's the best feeling in the world when, creatively, everything aligns in a band. But it's equally satisfying when attitudinally you all know you've reached the same place; by the time we started working on *Strangeways*, we all knew we had nothing left to prove – not to the world, not even to each other. That gives you an immense confidence, but it also relieves some of the pressure. We still wanted to *impress* one another of course, but by doing so in a more relaxed environment allowed more room for the magic to happen.

By 1987 we had released bestselling albums, toured the world, received critical acclaim beyond our dreams and had a devoted fanbase like no other. But we no longer felt like we had to *chase* it. I felt fulfilled and happy.

Strangeways felt like pure musical instinct. It was unusual. Lush. Atmospheric. Cinematic. Everything just *poured* into that record. The promise of what we had been building to. We weren't trying to force anything and subsequently there were no compromises. Nothing felt like it needed fixing. There's a good reason why we were done with it within a few months.

Unlike before, the album was less about potential singles. We were more interested in a soundscape and a cohesion. *Strangeways* captured that better than anything we'd done. A lot of it came together in the studio and, in a good way, I think you can hear that. As a closing chapter, where everything just comes together, it's perfect. Johnny possibly aside, we just didn't know we were working on the closing chapter. The productive, good-humoured sessions masked a lot. I don't think we really appreciated quite how burned-out Johnny was really feeling.

He took his desire to experiment to a new level on *Strangeways*. There was a keyboard in the studio called an Emulator II. The original Emulator was one of the first samplers. The second model in Wool Hall was renowned for its greater depth of orchestral sounds which provided Johnny with the opportunity to come up with the most incredible virtuoso parts for many of the songs on the album. As there was no way Rough Trade would have paid for a real string section to be brought into the studio, Johnny just 'Emulated' them. When I say, 'just', I'm really doing him an injustice. I remember sitting down behind him when he was playing around with string ideas for 'Last Night I Dreamt That Somebody Loved Me' and thinking – *hold on, when the hell did you learn how to do that?*

It was the same for the piano parts on the opening track, 'A Rush and a Push and the Land Is Ours'. It was quite an experience to just watch his dexterity as a musician bring so much new instrumentation to the table. He was a musical polymath. After every take in the main studio, we'd go upstairs to the control room to hear how it was sounding. Halfway up the staircase was an old, battered string instrument called an autoharp. Each time we went past it, we would always give it a playful strum. Of course, Johnny got hold of it – I think Streety might have suggested using it at some point – and removed it from its previous ornamental status and sat down in the control room to see if he could tease anything out of it. He could. The result was 'I Won't Share You', one of the most beautiful tunes you're ever to likely hear, a song of such splendour knocked out just like that, almost in passing.

We finished the album in April and on the day the mixing was complete, we grabbed a beer, dimmed the lights and all sat down in the studio with Stephen for the playback session of what we had just created. I have rarely experienced a better feeling than what I experienced that night. Just a matter of weeks before – just two months earlier – this album didn't exist. Now I was listening to the most incredible body of work that, with Stephen's help, we had crafted together. We had nothing and then we had magic. Boy, did it sound good.

After we split up, people suggested that *Strangeways* always sounded like the product of a band about to fall apart, saying stuff like, 'You

Me and Rourkey outside Wool Hall Studios the morning after finishing *Strangeways*.

know, if you listen to the album, you can hear the cracks.' This is bol-
locks. The album is the result of remarkable time spent in the studio.
With *Strangeways*, it felt like we were making an album *for us* – it was our
Sgt. Pepper. And I know this because I was fucking there.

During the recording of *Strangeways*, I felt that my own musicianship
was starting to edge a little bit closer towards Johnny's and Andy's. Do you
have any idea what it's like to be the third component in a power trio with
Andy Rourke and Johnny fucking Marr? But I never felt more comfortable
at a session than I did at those. And making sure you're in the right space
mentally will only improve your physical performance. I was in such a
good place when we were making this record that I have no doubt that
it worked to my advantage as a drummer who worked off confidence.

There was no planned tour or promotional campaign for *Strangeways,
Here We Come*, at least not that I was aware of. After the album was
recorded, there wasn't any kind of coordinated effort to promote it live
and it's a huge regret of mine that we never played those songs together

240

on a stage. Truth be told, none of this was a great surprise as *Strangeways* was released as our final contractual studio album with Rough Trade. We had signed to major label EMI at the end of the previous year. It was also around this time that we played what would turn out to be our last-ever gig at London's Brixton Academy on 12 December as part of an Artists Against Apartheid benefit. But of course we didn't know that then.

I always wonder what the follow-up to *Strangeways* would have sounded like if we hadn't split up. I still think about it a lot. It's the great 'What if?', isn't it? As a band, there is always the desire to maintain the core essence of the group with each new album while ensuring there is enough progression to keep things interesting. I'm confident we did that. But where we would have gone next? Who knows.

That fateful day came in July 1987 – halfway between completing *Strangeways* and releasing it – when Johnny called a meeting with all of us at Geales fish and chip restaurant in Notting Hill and announced he was leaving the band.

Tensions had risen since the end of the of the *Strangeways* sessions. We'd recorded a few B-sides for 'Girlfriend in a Coma', which Johnny wasn't too enamoured with and a new manager who would help alleviate some of the business pressure from our twenty-three-year-old guitarist had lasted fewer than six weeks, but it was still shocking. Given what we had just achieved and what we were about to release to the world, it made even less sense. There had been no blow-up, no arguments, no ultimatums. I know others might have a different interpretation as to how this played out – and there was of course much debating in the press – but all I know is that I would have done anything I could to keep the band going in its only true iteration. It had been the best part of five relentless years of work in which time the Smiths truly became one of the best bands in the world. We *all* needed a break. But it didn't have to be a permanent one.

I suggested recording one more album, desperate to cling on to what we had. Johnny just said, 'No.'

It was the only thing I could think of in that moment. I was floundering, just trying to keep it together. It's a bit like the end of relationship. One side of the partnership has lived with the consequences of their decision and impending action long before they show their hand. And when it is eventually revealed to the blindsided party, it is only natural for *them* to suggest a compromise. 'Let's give it six months and try and work things out' is rarely a practical solution at that point. But that's how I felt.

When someone leaves a relationship, some people immediately seek out something to fill that void, to replicate the comfort and familiarity they lost. It's the rebound effect – you try to recreate what you had. To that extent, while we'd lost a quarter of the thing we loved, we still had three-quarters left. We told ourselves, 'Well, we've still got *most* of it.'

X

We booked a session at Power Plant studios in Willesden, London, with me, Andy and Morrissey to try out a replacement after Johnny's departure. We brought in Stephen Street to resume his recording duties. Morrissey suggested that we draft in Ivor Perry on guitar. I'd met Ivor before when his band Easterhouse opened for the Smiths in Scotland in 1985 and more recently he'd formed a group called the Cradle with Craig Gannon.

I was up for giving it a try. You never know if someone will click creatively. Sometimes it works brilliantly, sometimes it doesn't. Visually, Ivor looked great, so at least that was a start!

When we started playing, it sounded okay. Not bad, not amazing – just *okay*. We worked on an instrumental that didn't really go anywhere and an early version of 'Bengali in Platforms' that Morrissey returned to for his first solo album *Viva Hate*, but it sounded nothing like the final version at that point. It wasn't a matter of technical ability with Ivor – he could clearly play – but it didn't have the spark that we were hoping for. It must have been quite awkward for Ivor all things considered.

We weren't consciously looking for a like-for-like replacement for Johnny; it's impossible to fill those boots. But that said, we certainly knew the size of his boots.

I couldn't grasp the finality of Johnny's departure. The deflation and sadness that came with the loss of not only my bandmate but also dear friend was almost physically debilitating at times. I saw Johnny pretty much every day from late 1982 to 1986. And I mean *every* day. So I was mourning his departure from my life. To call it a bereavement might sound dramatic, but that's how I felt. In my heavy heart I knew it was irrevocably over.

Almost immediately it felt like I had the role of consigliere bestowed upon me by Morrissey – although 'fixer' might have been closer to the truth. Somebody to have the difficult conversations on his behalf. On that first day back in the studio, Moz gave me the eye over dinner and we left the room. He told me he didn't want one of the guys from the studio who was eating dinner with us to be present and that *I* should ask him to leave. Similarly, when it quickly became aware that it was not going to work out with Ivor, Morrissey asked me to break the news to him myself.

'I don't think it's right coming from me as it was you that invited him along to the session in the first place,' I told Morrissey.

Morrissey said, 'I just *can't* be the one who relieves Ivor of his duties.'

That evening, I called Ivor from the hotel we were staying at. I thanked him for giving it his best shot but explained it just wasn't working out as we'd hoped. He was furious. Not because he hadn't got the gig, but mainly because Morrissey hadn't told him himself. He yelled, 'Why are you telling me this? Morrissey should be!'

Ivor told me he was going round to see Morrissey's that night to 'kick his fucking head in'.

After the session was aborted, I didn't hear from Morrissey for a number of days. It started to sink in pretty quickly that it was over so I decided to release a statement announcing my departure. The music press ran speculative stories of rumour and counter-rumour for the rest of the year based on hearsay. But one thing was for certain, the headline was true:

'SMITHS TO SPLIT'

I contacted Morrissey through Pat Bellis who worked at Rough Trade and told her to convey to him that if he ever wanted to work together again then maybe in a few years he could drop me a line.

X

Seventeen months later, I got a message from Morrissey.

He needed a drummer. And, as it turned out, a bass player and a guitarist as well. This is how me, Andy and Craig ended up back at the Wool Hall at the end of 1988.

Stephen Street was also there of course, not only on production duties again, but also as Mozzer's key songwriting partner. He had co-written every track on *Viva Hate*, Morrissey's debut solo album that had been released to great critical and commercial acclaim in March.

Strangely, it didn't feel like a dramatic reunion. Maybe too much time had passed. Maybe not *enough*. But it did feel very natural. We recorded Morrissey's next two singles – 'Last of the Famous International Playboys' and 'Interesting Drug' – in quick succession.

Talk soon turned to the possibility of a gig. There has always been some debate as to whether the show was also meant as an unofficial farewell to the Smiths or the start of Morrissey's live solo career. And I suppose there is a bit of truth to the former with half of the eight songs performed being Smiths numbers and the other half solo material. But it was Morrissey's show now. We weren't trying to recreate the Smiths exactly; we were just doing something new but familiar for that one night.

We agreed that as a mark of respect to Johnny, we wouldn't have any songs in the set that we'd previously played live with him.

The show was scheduled for 22 December 1988 at the Civic Hall in Wolverhampton. It was meant to be a one-off. We didn't do it with the intention of launching a tour. It was just something special. And as such there was no entrance fee. Instead, sporting a Morrissey or Smiths T-shirt was all that was required for admission.

The auditorium was jammed way past fire safety limits. To say the crowd were 'enthusiastic' would be the greatest understatement ever uttered from my lips. It was bedlam: Morrissey was under siege from the first number – 'Stop Me If You Think You've Heard This One Before' – as fan after fan scrambled over each other and threw themselves at him, desperate to touch or caress him for however fleeting a moment. It was like the rebirth of Christ and they were his rabid apostles. Bedlam became hysteria.

At first, I thought it was an incredible sight to behold. But when it became apparent that it wasn't going to subside, I got a bit frustrated with the proceedings. That level of fan intensity is a rare, beautiful thing. To a point. But Morrissey's microphone was constantly ripped from his hands, guitar pedals were being smashed, leads were pulled out from Andy's bass and Craig's guitar. It was carnage.

At one point during the set, it was just vocals and drums as the mayhem that ensued had rendered Andy's and Craig's playing untenable. I've watched parts of it since and, however special an event it was, it's also evident to see my frustration during some of the set.

It would be the last time that Morrissey, Andy and I all performed on the same stage together in front of an audience.

We reunited several weeks later to shoot Morrissey's 'film' for his single, 'The Last of the Famous International Playboys'. I say 'film' as Moz did not and would not make 'videos', the very notion being abhorrent to him. 'Film' was class, 'film' was elegance. Film was shot on real celluloid.

The 'filming' took place in an old London theatre. There were a load of people and crew milling around the place. There was a camera on a boom, criss-crossing in front of me. I became uncharacteristically aware of my jug ears and because of this, I asked the director Tim Broad if I could be filmed from the side. He couldn't hear what I was saying as there were so many people about. I repeated myself, saying I wanted this angle as I was a bit paranoid about the size of my ears. 'I'd rather it be a side shot,' I sheepishly said again. Tim looked at me quizzically, then said, 'I'm sorry, Mike, I can't hear you.' In obvious frustration, he turned away from the band to face all the onlookers. 'Can everybody just fucking shut up? I'm trying to listen to Mike talk,' he boomed. Suddenly, it was pin-drop silence: the director had thrown a fucking wobbler. The schoolteacher was shouting at everybody. I thought, *Shall I even mention it again?*

Tim turned back to me. 'Sorry, Mike, what was that you said?' A pregnant hush engulfed the place. Horrified and embarrassed at now having to make this request in front of such an enraptured crowd, I squawked, 'I was just saying that I don't really want a camera shot directly in front of me. I'd rather have it on the side.' Tim scrunched up his face quizzically before replying, 'Why is that?'

Andy broke the silence and shouted at the top of his voice:

'Because he's got fucking massive ears!'

EPILOGUE

Andy moved to New York around 2009 as he felt stifled in the Manchester scene. I thought it could be a really good move, a fresh start for one of the UK's best bass players. Andy had a radio show on East Village Radio in NY. There was a pizza place that he used to visit – Frank's, a proper Italian spot. The building next to it was East Village Radio, with a glass front that opened out onto the street.

I think Andy had just popped in one day, got chatting and they asked him to do a bit of DJing. I stood in for one of his shows and I was invited to have a regular weekly slot on the station. I said that I would love to. Of course, Andy broadcast his show from the station, but unfortunately their budget didn't stretch to fly me over from the UK every week, so I recorded my show here and sent it over.

We Skyped each other periodically, but Andy was shit at that kind of thing.

The conversation normally went something like this:

'Hi mate, how's it going?'
Andy: 'Great, how are you?'
'Great! What have you been up to?'
Andy: 'Oh this and that.'
'Oh right. What's this and that then?'
Andy: 'Oh you know, just the usual.'

'Oh, come on man, you live in New York for fuck's sake. Give us some detail of what's happening out there.'

Andy: 'Just hanging out, I suppose.'

'Right, okay.'

Andy struggled at communicating over a screen, but sit down face to face with him and he would light up. And that's exactly what would happen when he used to come over occasionally to the UK. We'd hook up and chew the fat. No matter how long it had been since our last catch-up, we always instantly fell back into that rhythm that we had experienced from our very first-ever meeting in Drone Studios.

A few years later, Andy called me from New York and told me that he'd been diagnosed with pancreatic cancer. He informed me that there were two types and that he'd got the 'good' one, if there is such a thing. He revealed that he was having a major operation called the 'Whipple' procedure, which would remove part of his non-vital organs to stop the spread of the disease. He asked me to keep it quiet as he didn't really want it to be common knowledge. Of course I would, I told him. I tried to reassure him and tell him everything was going to be okay, but in reality, how could I possibly know that? I was in deep shock. I really didn't know *what* to say.

The next time he came over to Britain, we met up in a bar in Manchester. He was there with Francesca, a lovely woman whom he'd met in NY and subsequently married.

When I laid eyes on him, I burst into tears. I was so happy to see him. To my surprise, he looked great. He told me about the treatment and suchlike. We had a laugh as usual, but I was still really scared for him. I was relieved there had been some sort of progress, some sort of respite, but you always fear that aggressive re-emergence.

I later heard that the cancer was back, but this time the prognosis was not so good.

It was hard to know who knew and who didn't – he asked me not to tell anyone. I remember seeing his adopted daughter Martene in Manchester after he was first diagnosed. She asked me how I was and I said I was fine. Then she asked if I'd seen her dad and I said yes, he seemed okay. But I got the sense she didn't know and I didn't want to say anything in case he hadn't told her yet. Later, Andy mentioned I had bumped into her and thanked me for not saying anything. It turned out he'd told her not to tell anyone either. Neither of us brought it up, which he appreciated – it showed how private he wanted to keep things.

Later, I'd hear bits of news from friends who had seen him or visited. Some said he didn't look too well and others said things might have taken a more dramatic turn. From the beginning, he told me the average life expectancy after diagnosis was around three years. I'd heard of people living fifteen or twenty years and I encouraged him to focus on hope, not statistics.

I didn't get in touch with him as much as I wanted to as I was worried I would be encroaching upon his life when he needed rest and whatever quality moments of respite he had with his wife. In late 2022, I saw a picture of him online at what looked like an awards ceremony. He'd lost a lot of weight and looked very frail. The comments under the picture were quite complimentary about his weight loss, as nobody outside of his family and very close friends knew anything of his situation.

That's when I flew over to see him. He mentioned going to the hospital every couple of days and was surprised that they hadn't kept him in. He wasn't in a hospice but he had entered the palliative care stage. I wondered how much time he had left.

In February 2023, Tina and I decided we had to go over and visit him, whether he wanted to see me or not. I called him and gave him some bullshit story about us having a holiday break in New York and how it would be nice for us to hook up and say hello while we were out there.

We arrived in New York and the following day took the subway over to Andy's. I was aghast to see that he lived on the fifth floor of a building without a lift. Even though I was in relatively good cardio shape, I was still out of breath by the time I got to his door. I could not imagine someone undergoing the kind of intensive treatment Andy was having to also have to navigate such a climb on a regular basis.

When I entered his apartment, he didn't look at all well. Anybody who's spoken to someone in a critical condition knows that the conversation is very stilted as you don't want to say the wrong thing.

The one thing that we did talk about – and I'm so glad we did – was what he became famous for: his bass playing. Most musicians want recognition for their art. Most of the time that just happens on a minor level. Only a very small percentage manage it on an international level.

Andy achieved that. He was part of something bigger than the four of us. But the sound we made, with his indelible, individual contribution, would not have been the same without him. People quite rightly praise Johnny's playing, but the *sound* of the Smiths was just as much Andy. I feel incredibly lucky to have had the opportunity to play with such a brilliant musician.

When I received the call in May 2023 to say he'd passed away, it was still shocking, even though I had been waiting for – and dreading – that call. After the last time of seeing him in New York, I still hoped that there would be some new treatment, some untried miracle cure they could administer. I said to Tina, 'You never know.' But she did know. And I did really. He didn't have long left but I just couldn't accept that.

Even now, it still feels quite surreal talking about Andy in the past tense. But I've found solace in the knowledge that I was lucky to have worked with him and called him my mate.

Cheers Rourkey.

X

Back in 1982 when I first met those lads Johnny and Steven for that audition in Spirit Studios on Tariff Street in Manchester, I would never have imagined that, nearly fifty years later, I would be sitting where I am today, talking about my time in the Smiths. Looking back, everything fell into place *really* quickly after that meeting. A year later, by the end of 1983, we had signed with Rough Trade, recorded a session for John Peel and performed on *Top of the Pops*. All within twelve months. Unbelievable.

Ultimately, we were four working-class lads from Manchester, but we built something truly unique and for a short time we were completely unstoppable. I will never tire of people coming up to me and saying, 'I love the Smiths! The band completely changed my life!' Yeah, mine too!

I've experienced some pretty trying, well-documented moments in my career, but the great times far outweigh the bad and as I said at the start of this book, I will always focus on the positives. And with the Smiths, I was just lucky enough to get together with a pair of supernaturally talented musicians and the best frontperson and lyricist I've ever worked with. I wasn't just playing the drums in a band. The Smiths became my whole life.

I was DJing in Italy a few months ago and a guy came up to me and said, 'Hey Mike, any chance of an autograph? I'm the biggest Smiths fan in the world.'

To which I replied with total sincerity, 'After me, that is.'

ACKNOWLEDGEMENTS

Massive thanks to Jen 'the Otts' Bickerdike for convincing me to do this in the first place, and her subsequent encouragement, advice and tireless dedication.

Also a thank you to Ben Smith and Jon Beckley at F-10 for being the facilitator.

My manager Danny Watson, whose brilliant mind and seemingly bottomless knowledge of everything music-related (and beyond) has been invaluable in helping me navigate through obstacles galore over the years.

Thanks to Pete Selby, James Lilford, Dusty Miller and all at New Modern who've helped with the production of the book.

Thanks to all who joined me in my story including, but not exclusively: Ian Chambers, Steve Mardy, Andy Farley, Joe Moody, Wes Graham, Pete Hope, Foxy, Phil Powell, Joe Moss, John Peel, John Porter, Stephen Street and a special thank you to my fellow Smiths.

The team at New Modern would like to thank the following individuals:

Sarah Meaney for copy-editing
Peter Stoneman for editorial support
Nige Tassell for proofreading
Marie Doherty for typesetting
Paul Palmer-Edwards for cover design
Amanda Russell for image research
Dusty Miller for publicity
Charlotte Rose, Andreina Brezzo and the team
at Simon & Schuster UK for sales and distribution